Estate Planning for Blended Families

Navigating the Legal and Tax Implications of Trusts, Estates, and Gift Tax in Complex Family Structures

Miles Hawkins

Table of Contents

1 Understanding Blended Families

The modern family has evolved significantly. What was once considered traditional – a nuclear family with two biological parents – is now just one of many family structures. Blended families, formed through remarriage or repartnering, are increasingly common, bringing unique complexities to estate planning. These families often consist of two separate family units merging, each with its own history, assets, and expectations. Children may have different biological parents, step-parents, half-siblings, and step-siblings, creating a network of relationships that require careful consideration when planning for the future. Understanding these dynamics is the first step towards effective estate planning in a blended family context. Navigating the legal and tax implications requires a sensitive and tailored approach. It's crucial to recognize that estate planning for blended families isn't simply about distributing assets; it's about safeguarding family harmony and ensuring that everyone feels valued and protected.

One of the most pressing challenges in estate planning for blended families is balancing the interests of various family members. Spouses may wish to provide for each other while also ensuring that their own children from previous relationships are adequately cared for. This can create tension, particularly if there are significant disparities in assets or if one spouse feels that their children are being unfairly disadvantaged. Consider a scenario where one spouse enters a marriage with substantial wealth accumulated over years of work, while the other spouse has limited assets. Upon the first spouse's death, their children from a previous marriage may be concerned about their inheritance being shared with the surviving spouse and their children. Similar concerns can arise regarding the distribution of assets if the surviving spouse remarries. These complex dynamics necessitate open communication and careful planning to avoid potential conflicts and ensure a fair distribution of assets according to the wishes of both spouses.

Another key challenge arises from the varying legal rights and obligations within blended families. Step-parents generally do not have the same legal rights and responsibilities towards stepchildren as biological parents. This can affect decisions regarding guardianship, healthcare, and inheritance. For instance, a step-parent may not automatically have the legal authority to make medical decisions for a stepchild, and they may not be entitled to inherit from a stepchild who dies intestate (without a will). This legal distinction underscores the importance of formalizing intentions through wills, trusts, and other legal documents. Without proper planning, the distribution of assets may not align with the wishes of the family members, leading to unintended consequences and potential disputes.

Pre-nuptial agreements play a crucial role in clarifying financial expectations and protecting individual assets in blended families. These agreements, established before marriage, outline the ownership and division of property in the event of divorce or death. For individuals entering a second or subsequent marriage, a pre-nuptial agreement can provide clarity and security, ensuring that assets accumulated prior to the marriage are protected for their children from previous relationships. This is particularly important when one spouse has significantly more assets than the other or when there are complex family dynamics involved. A well-drafted pre-nuptial agreement can prevent misunderstandings and potential conflict down the road, offering peace of mind to all parties involved. Beyond the financial aspects, pre-nuptial agreements can address issues such as spousal support, estate planning, and the division of assets acquired during the marriage. They can also specify how pre-marital debts will be handled. By addressing these issues upfront, couples can establish a clear understanding of their financial obligations and protect themselves from potential financial burdens. It's important to note that pre-nuptial agreements should be created with the involvement of legal counsel for both parties to ensure fairness and enforceability. Open communication and transparency during this process are essential for building trust and fostering a strong foundation for the marriage.

Within the broader context of estate planning, blended families benefit from utilizing a variety of legal tools to achieve their objectives. Wills, trusts, and powers of attorney are essential instruments for directing the distribution of assets and ensuring that wishes are carried out. These documents provide a legal framework for managing finances, healthcare decisions, and guardianship arrangements, particularly in situations involving minor children or individuals with special needs. Without these legal mechanisms, the distribution of assets may be subject to state intestacy laws, which may not align with the family's intentions. Therefore, establishing clear legal directives is crucial for protecting the interests of all family members and avoiding potential legal complications. Proactive planning and open communication are key to navigating the complexities of estate planning for blended families and securing their financial future. By addressing potential challenges head-on and utilizing the appropriate legal tools, families can ensure that their assets are protected and their wishes are respected.

1.1 Defining the Modern Family

The traditional nuclear family, once the dominant model in many societies, has evolved. Today, the landscape of kinship is far more diverse, encompassing a multitude of structures. We see multi-generational households, single-parent families, adoptive families, and, increasingly, blended families. This chapter focuses specifically on the latter, exploring the multifaceted nature of the modern blended family and the implications for estate planning. A blended family, at its core, is formed when two individuals unite in a committed relationship, bringing with them children from previous relationships. This merging of two distinct family units creates a unique dynamic, often characterized by a rich tapestry of relationships and interconnectedness. These connections, while often a source of strength and love, can also present unique challenges when it comes to planning for the future, particularly in the realm of estate planning.

Blended families can take many forms. We might see a married couple where one spouse has children from a prior relationship, while the other does not. Another common scenario involves both partners entering the marriage with children from previous unions. In some instances, the couple may choose to have children together, further enriching the complexity of the family structure. There are also situations where children reside primarily with one parent, visiting the other parent and their new family periodically. Each of these variations carries its own unique set of circumstances, emphasizing the need for customized estate planning solutions tailored to the specific needs and dynamics of the family in question.

One key aspect of the modern blended family that distinguishes it from the traditional nuclear family is the presence of step-parents and step-children. These relationships, often formed through circumstance rather than biology, can be both rewarding and complex. The legal ties between step-parents and step-children are typically less clearly defined than those between biological parents and children. This lack of automatic legal recognition can have significant implications when it comes to inheritance and decision-making, particularly in situations involving medical emergencies or incapacity. Without proper estate planning, step-children may be inadvertently excluded from inheritance or lack the legal authority to make decisions on behalf of a step-parent. Similarly, step-parents may not have the automatic right to make medical decisions for step-children in the absence of explicit legal documentation.

Further complicating matters is the potential for strained relationships between biological parents who are no longer together. While many blended families enjoy positive co-parenting relationships, lingering tensions from previous relationships can impact estate planning decisions. One parent may harbor concerns about their assets ultimately benefiting their ex-spouse's new family, leading to disagreements about inheritance distribution. These dynamics underscore the importance of open communication, clear expectations, and legal guidance in navigating the complexities of estate planning for blended families. A well-drafted estate plan can serve as a neutral framework for managing these challenges and ensuring that the wishes of all parties are respected.

Another distinctive characteristic of blended families is the potential for disparate financial circumstances. Partners entering a blended family may have vastly different levels of wealth, income, and pre-existing financial obligations. One partner may have significant assets accumulated prior to the relationship, while the other may have limited resources. These differences can create challenges in determining equitable distribution of assets and ensuring that all children, both biological and step-children, are adequately provided for. Pre-nuptial agreements can be a valuable tool in addressing these disparities and establishing clear financial boundaries before marriage. These agreements can help protect individual assets, clarify inheritance expectations, and minimize potential conflict down the line. For example, a pre-nuptial agreement might stipulate that each partner's pre-marital assets remain separate property and that any inheritance received during the marriage will be considered separate property as well. This can provide a framework for managing finances and ensuring that each partner's pre-existing financial obligations are respected.

The complexity of family structures further necessitates a detailed consideration of healthcare directives and powers of attorney. Who will make medical decisions if a parent becomes incapacitated? Who will manage finances if a partner is unable to do so? These are crucial questions that must be addressed proactively in the estate plan. In blended families, these decisions can be especially sensitive, given the potential for differing opinions among family members. For instance, a biological parent may have different views on medical treatment than a step-parent. Clear documentation through healthcare directives and powers of attorney can provide guidance and minimize the potential for disputes during challenging times. These documents can specify who has the authority to make medical and financial decisions, ensuring that the wishes of the incapacitated individual are respected and that their well-being is protected. This careful consideration of all potential scenarios is crucial in creating a comprehensive and effective estate plan for blended families.

1.2 Unique Planning Challenges

Blended families often encounter a distinct set of estate planning hurdles absent in traditional family structures. These challenges arise from the complex web of relationships, varying financial circumstances, and the potential for conflict among family members. Successfully navigating these complexities requires careful consideration, open communication, and a tailored estate plan designed to address the specific needs and dynamics of the blended family unit. One common challenge is balancing the interests of multiple sets of children. Biological children may have expectations regarding their inheritance, while stepchildren may also be considered part of the family and deserving of provisions. This balancing act can create tension and requires careful consideration of each child's needs and the parents' overall wishes.

Another significant challenge stems from the disparate financial situations that individuals bring into a blended family. One spouse may have significantly more assets than the other, or one spouse may have children from a previous marriage who are financially dependent. These differences can complicate estate planning decisions, particularly regarding the distribution of assets and the allocation of resources for education, healthcare, and other needs. Furthermore, pre-existing financial obligations, such as alimony or child support, can impact the overall estate plan and must be carefully considered.

Integrating pre-existing estate plans into a new, unified plan is also a crucial undertaking. Each spouse likely entered the blended family with an estate plan designed for their previous family structure. These plans might include wills, trusts, and beneficiary designations that may no longer align with the current family situation. Reconciling these pre-existing plans with the new blended family's needs and goals requires careful review and modification. Neglecting this integration can lead to unintended consequences and conflict after a spouse's death.

The presence of step-parents introduces another layer of complexity. Step-parents often develop strong emotional bonds with their stepchildren, but they may not have the same legal rights and responsibilities as biological parents. This can create challenges in ensuring that stepchildren are adequately provided for in the event of a step-parent's death, especially if the biological parent predeceases the step-parent. Properly addressing this requires exploring various legal tools, such as adoption, guardianship designations, or trusts specifically designed for the benefit of stepchildren.

Estate planning in blended families is further complicated by the potential for disagreements and conflict among family members. Differing opinions on asset distribution, inheritance expectations, and the role of step-parents can strain relationships and lead to disputes. Open communication and transparency are crucial for mitigating these potential conflicts. Family meetings to discuss estate planning intentions can help manage expectations and ensure everyone understands the reasoning behind the chosen strategies.

Establishing clear and well-defined roles and responsibilities within the blended family is also essential for successful estate planning. Determining who will manage finances, make healthcare decisions, and handle other important matters can help prevent misunderstandings and conflict. These roles should be documented in legal documents such as powers of attorney and healthcare directives, ensuring a smooth transition in the event of incapacity or death.

Addressing the potential for future changes in family dynamics is another key aspect of estate planning for blended families. Children may grow up and become financially independent, relationships may evolve, and new family members may be added through birth or adoption. The estate plan should be flexible enough to accommodate these changes without requiring significant revisions. Regularly reviewing and updating the plan can ensure that it continues to align with the family's evolving needs and circumstances.

The emotional dynamics of blended families require careful consideration. Feelings of favoritism, jealousy, and resentment can arise, particularly when it comes to the distribution of assets. Acknowledging these emotional undercurrents and addressing them proactively can help minimize conflict and preserve family relationships. Engaging a therapist or family counselor can provide a neutral space for family members to discuss their concerns and work towards a mutually agreeable estate plan. Furthermore, seeking professional legal and financial advice is crucial for navigating the complexities of estate planning in blended families. An experienced estate planning attorney can provide guidance on the appropriate legal tools and strategies for achieving the family's goals while minimizing potential conflict and tax implications. A financial advisor can assist in creating a comprehensive financial plan that complements the estate plan, ensuring that the family's financial resources are managed effectively.

Finally, maintaining accurate and up-to-date records is vital. This includes keeping track of assets, liabilities, beneficiary designations, and other relevant documents. Organized records simplify the estate administration process and help avoid confusion and disputes after a spouse's death. Utilizing digital tools and secure storage can facilitate record-keeping and ensure easy access for all relevant parties. In conclusion, estate planning for blended families presents unique challenges that require careful attention and proactive planning. By understanding these challenges, engaging in open communication, seeking professional guidance, and implementing appropriate legal and financial strategies, blended families can create an estate plan that protects their assets, provides for their loved ones, and preserves family harmony for generations to come.

1.3 Pre-nuptial Agreements

A pre-nuptial agreement, often referred to as a pre-nup, is a legally binding contract created by a couple before they marry. It outlines the ownership of assets and how they will be divided in the event of a divorce or death. For blended families, pre-nups offer a crucial layer of protection, safeguarding the interests of both spouses and their respective children from previous relationships. Consider it a proactive measure, not a sign of pessimism, but rather a practical approach to protecting pre-marital assets, inheritances, and future earnings. This clarity can significantly reduce potential conflict and emotional distress should the marriage dissolve.

A pre-nuptial agreement establishes clear financial boundaries, ensuring that each spouse's pre-marital assets remain separate. This is particularly important in blended families where one or both partners bring substantial assets, businesses, or inheritances into the marriage. Without a pre-nup, these assets could become commingled marital property, subject to division in a divorce. The agreement can also delineate how assets acquired during the marriage will be handled. This clarity can help prevent misunderstandings and disputes later on, especially regarding the distribution of assets to children from previous relationships.

Protecting inheritance rights of children from prior relationships is a paramount concern in blended families. A pre-nup can ensure that children from a previous marriage receive their intended inheritance, preventing unintended consequences stemming from state intestacy laws or claims from the new spouse. The agreement can stipulate that specific assets, like a family business or a vacation home, are earmarked for the children's future benefit, irrespective of the marital outcome. This offers considerable peace of mind, ensuring that the children's financial well-being is secured.

Addressing financial obligations and support is another key function of a pre-nuptial agreement. It can define the responsibilities of each spouse regarding spousal support (alimony) in the event of a divorce. This can include limitations on the amount and duration of payments, providing financial predictability for both parties. Furthermore, the agreement can address the financial responsibilities towards children from prior relationships, outlining child support obligations and ensuring that the pre-nup does not negatively impact existing court-ordered support arrangements. Navigating the complexities of estate planning for blended families requires careful consideration of how pre-marital assets and inheritances will be handled after death. A pre-nuptial agreement can specify how these assets will be distributed, overriding default state laws that might not align with the couple's wishes. This can be especially relevant in situations involving complex family dynamics, such as step-parent adoptions or significant age differences between spouses. The agreement ensures that each spouse's estate plan reflects their individual intentions, preserving family legacies and providing for loved ones according to their specific desires.

Developing a comprehensive and legally sound pre-nuptial agreement requires the expertise of qualified legal counsel. Each spouse should consult with their own attorney to ensure they fully understand the terms and implications of the agreement. This independent legal advice safeguards each party's individual interests and ensures that the agreement is fair and equitable. Open communication and transparency throughout the process are essential. Couples should discuss their financial situations honestly and openly, addressing any concerns or questions they may have. This collaborative approach fosters trust and understanding, laying the foundation for a strong and stable financial future for the blended family.

Beyond the financial aspects, a well-drafted pre-nup can provide clarity and peace of mind, facilitating open communication about financial matters within the family. By addressing potentially sensitive issues beforehand, a pre-nup can help mitigate conflict and strengthen the family unit. It provides a framework for financial decision-making, fostering transparency and trust between spouses, and ultimately promoting a more harmonious family dynamic.

Incorporating a pre-nuptial agreement into the overall estate plan for a blended family is a proactive step towards securing the financial future of all members involved. It offers a valuable tool for protecting individual assets, inheritance rights, and ensuring that the unique needs of each spouse and their children are addressed. While it may require navigating potentially sensitive discussions, the long-term benefits of clarity, financial security, and potential conflict avoidance make the pre-nuptial agreement a crucial consideration for any blended family embarking on the journey of marriage and estate planning. By addressing potential financial challenges proactively, couples can build a stronger foundation for their future together, ensuring financial stability and harmony within their blended family.

2 Estate Planning Basics

Careful estate planning is crucial for all families, but it takes on a special significance for blended families. The presence of multiple sets of children, step-parents, and ex-spouses introduces a layer of complexity that requires thoughtful consideration and strategic planning. This chapter lays the groundwork for understanding the essential tools of estate planning—wills and the probate process—and how they apply specifically to the unique dynamics of blended families.

A will is a legally binding document that dictates how your assets will be distributed after your death. It allows you to name guardians for minor children, specify who will manage your estate, and most importantly, determine who receives your property. Without a will, your estate will be distributed according to the laws of intestacy in your state, which may not align with your wishes and can create unintended consequences, particularly within a blended family structure. For example, your assets might be divided equally among your biological children, potentially excluding your stepchildren entirely. A well-drafted will ensures that your intentions are clearly stated, minimizing the potential for disputes and providing for all intended beneficiaries.

Crafting a will requires careful consideration of your family's unique circumstances. In a blended family, you might want to provide for both your current spouse and children from a previous marriage. You can allocate specific assets to particular individuals, create trusts to manage inheritance for minor or special needs children, or establish a framework for dividing the estate fairly among all family members. It's essential to work with an experienced estate planning attorney who understands the nuances of blended families and can help you draft a will that reflects your wishes and safeguards the interests of everyone involved.

The probate process is the legal procedure that follows death, involving the validation of your will and the administration of your estate. During probate, the court oversees the payment of debts, the identification and valuation of assets, and the distribution of inheritance according to the terms of the will (or intestacy laws if there is no will). This process can be time-consuming, expensive, and emotionally taxing for families, especially blended families where existing tensions might be exacerbated by inheritance disputes.

Probate can become particularly complex in blended families due to the potential for disagreements among family members. Different expectations regarding inheritance, competing claims on assets, and pre-existing family conflicts can lead to lengthy legal battles and strain relationships. Furthermore, the public nature of probate means that financial details become part of the public record, potentially creating unwanted scrutiny and discomfort for the family.

Fortunately, there are strategies to minimize the burden of probate, such as establishing a living trust, which we will discuss in a later chapter. However, even with a trust, certain assets may still pass through probate, so understanding the process is essential. Key aspects include identifying the executor named in the will, who is responsible for managing the estate, understanding the court procedures involved, and being aware of potential challenges that could arise. Preparing for probate in advance, by organizing financial records and communicating clearly with family members, can significantly ease the process and minimize the potential for conflict.

Specific state laws govern the probate process, so the details can vary. However, certain common elements include filing the will with the court, notifying beneficiaries and creditors, inventorying and appraising assets, paying outstanding debts and taxes, and ultimately distributing the remaining assets. Having a thorough understanding of these steps and working closely with an attorney throughout the process can help navigate the complexities of probate and ensure a smoother transition for your family.

While probate serves a crucial role in validating wills and ensuring legal distribution of assets, it's important to recognize its potential drawbacks, especially for blended families. The costs associated with court fees, legal representation, and executor compensation can significantly diminish the estate. The time involved can also be substantial, delaying the distribution of inheritance to beneficiaries. Moreover, the public nature of probate can expose family finances and potentially exacerbate existing conflicts.

For blended families, minimizing the assets that pass through probate can be particularly advantageous. This can be achieved through various estate planning tools, such as living trusts, joint ownership with rights of survivorship, and beneficiary designations on retirement accounts and life insurance policies. By strategically utilizing these tools, you can streamline the estate administration process, reduce costs, and maintain greater privacy for your family. Careful planning can also help mitigate potential disputes and ensure a smoother transition of assets, preserving family harmony during a difficult time.

Ultimately, understanding the basics of estate planning, including wills and the probate process, is the first step towards creating a secure and stable future for your blended family. By carefully considering your family's unique circumstances and working with experienced professionals, you can develop a comprehensive plan that protects your loved ones, minimizes potential conflicts, and ensures that your wishes are carried out according to your intentions.

2.1 Wills and Testaments

A will is a legal document that dictates your wishes regarding the distribution of your property and the care of any minor children after your death. It's a cornerstone of estate planning, providing you with the power to decide who receives your assets, minimizing potential family disputes and ensuring your wishes are respected. Without a valid will, your estate will be distributed according to your state's intestacy laws, which may not align with your intentions. These laws often prioritize spouses and biological children, potentially leaving stepchildren or other intended beneficiaries disinherited. Creating a will offers peace of mind, knowing you have taken proactive steps to secure your family's future.

Crafting a will involves several crucial components. First, you must clearly identify yourself and state your domicile. This establishes jurisdiction and avoids confusion. Then, you need to name an executor, the individual responsible for carrying out the instructions in your will. Choose someone trustworthy and capable of handling the administrative tasks involved. Contingency planning is important; name a successor executor in case your first choice is unable or unwilling to serve.

Next, you'll delineate the distribution of your assets. Be specific. Clearly identify beneficiaries by name and relationship and describe the property they are to receive. "To my son, John Smith, I leave my residence located at 123 Main Street." This level of detail prevents ambiguity and potential challenges to the will's validity. Consider including a residuary clause, a catch-all provision that designates a beneficiary for any assets not specifically mentioned in the will. This ensures that all of your property is accounted for.

For parents in blended families, addressing the guardianship of minor children is paramount. Your will allows you to nominate a guardian to care for your children in the event of your death. Consider not only the practicalities of care but also the emotional well-being of your children. Open communication with potential guardians is essential to ensure they understand and accept the responsibilities involved. While biological parents often have a preference, the ultimate decision rests with the court, considering the best interests of the child.

Witness requirements vary by state, but generally, two unrelated individuals must witness your signature and affirm that you are of sound mind and signing the will willingly. These witnesses play a crucial role in validating the document's authenticity. Seek legal counsel to ensure your will complies with your state's specific requirements regarding witness signatures and notarization. Proper execution is vital to avoid potential challenges to the will's validity after your passing.

Regularly reviewing and updating your will is crucial, particularly after significant life events such as marriage, divorce, the birth of a child, or a substantial change in your financial situation. These changes can impact your estate and necessitate adjustments to your will to reflect your current wishes. Failing to update your will can lead to unintended consequences and disputes among family members.

Finally, consider the interaction of your will with other estate planning tools. If you have established a trust, your will can work in conjunction with it, pouring over remaining assets into the trust after specific bequests are fulfilled. This coordinated approach can optimize asset distribution and minimize tax liabilities.

Creating a will isn't merely a legal formality; it's an act of love and responsibility. It provides clarity, minimizes potential conflict, and empowers you to shape the future for your loved ones. Seek professional guidance from an estate planning attorney. They can help you navigate the legal complexities, ensuring your will is legally sound and accurately reflects your wishes, providing peace of mind for you and your family. The small investment in legal counsel now can prevent significant headaches and heartache down the road. Remember, a well-drafted will isn't just about distributing assets; it's about preserving family harmony and honoring your legacy.

2.2 Probate Process

Death initiates a legal procedure called probate, the process by which a deceased person's will is validated (or the estate administered if there is no will), debts and taxes are settled, and the remaining assets are distributed to the beneficiaries. Understanding this process is crucial for blended families, as it can significantly impact how, when, and to whom assets are passed. Probate court oversight ensures a fair and legal distribution according to the will or state intestacy laws if no will exists. This process can be time-consuming, expensive, and emotionally draining, particularly for blended families with potentially competing interests among family members.

The initial step in probate involves validating the will. This includes verifying its legality, ensuring it meets state requirements, and confirming the testator's testamentary capacity—meaning they were of sound mind when creating the document. This step is vital in preventing fraud and ensuring the will accurately reflects the deceased's wishes. Without a valid will, the distribution of assets will be governed by the state's intestacy laws, which may not align with the deceased's intentions or the family's unique circumstances. In blended families, this can lead to unforeseen and potentially undesirable outcomes.

Following validation, an executor, named in the will or appointed by the court, takes charge of administering the estate. This individual is responsible for identifying, inventorying, and appraising all assets. The executor also pays outstanding debts, including taxes, medical bills, and funeral expenses. In blended families, the inventory and appraisal process can be particularly complex, potentially involving assets acquired during previous marriages or held jointly with individuals outside the immediate family. Careful documentation and clear communication among family members are crucial during this phase.

The complexity of the probate process is often amplified in blended families due to the potential for disputes among heirs. These disagreements can arise from various factors, including conflicting interpretations of the will, challenges to its validity, or differing expectations regarding asset distribution. Stepchildren, half-siblings, and former spouses may have competing claims, further complicating the probate proceedings. Open communication and clear documentation of the deceased's wishes can help mitigate these challenges, but it is essential to be prepared for the possibility of disputes.

While probate offers a structured framework for estate administration, it also comes with drawbacks, especially for blended families. The process is inherently public, meaning all records, including the will and inventory of assets, become part of the public record. This lack of privacy can be uncomfortable for some families. Moreover, probate can be costly, with expenses including court fees, executor fees, and attorney fees. These costs can quickly deplete estate assets, reducing the ultimate inheritance for beneficiaries. Finally, the probate process can be lengthy, often taking months or even years to complete. This delay can create financial hardship for beneficiaries who rely on those assets.

Navigating the probate process effectively requires careful planning and professional guidance. Consultations with an estate planning attorney are highly recommended, especially for blended families. An attorney can advise on strategies to minimize probate costs and delays, facilitate communication among family members, and ensure that the deceased's wishes are honored. Furthermore, they can help resolve disputes and navigate the complexities of state laws specific to probate. This advice can be invaluable in protecting the interests of all beneficiaries and facilitating a smoother transition during a difficult time.

A thorough understanding of the probate process is essential for blended families. By being aware of the steps involved, potential challenges, and available strategies to mitigate those challenges, families can better prepare for the legal and administrative tasks that follow the death of a loved one. Proactive planning and clear communication are key to navigating this complex process successfully and ensuring a fair and efficient distribution of assets. Early engagement with an estate planning attorney can provide invaluable support and guidance during this critical time, helping to minimize conflict and protect the interests of all involved parties. This proactive approach can ease the burden on grieving families and facilitate a more seamless transition in the aftermath of loss. Remember, the complexities of blended families require special attention to detail and careful consideration of all potential outcomes in estate planning.

3 Trusts for Blended Families

Blended families present unique estate planning challenges, often requiring sophisticated tools to ensure that assets are distributed according to the individual's wishes while minimizing potential conflict. Trusts, with their flexibility and control mechanisms, can be particularly valuable. One such tool is the revocable living trust, often called a living trust. This trust allows you to retain control over your assets during your lifetime, acting as both trustee and beneficiary. You can manage and use the property held within the trust as you normally would. Upon your death, the assets transfer seamlessly to your designated beneficiaries, bypassing the often lengthy and expensive probate process. This can be particularly beneficial in blended families, providing a quicker and more private distribution of assets. It also offers a level of control that a will cannot, allowing you to dictate precisely how and when assets are distributed to your beneficiaries, which could include specific provisions for both current and former spouses, as well as children from different marriages.

Irrevocable life insurance trusts (ILITs) offer a distinct advantage in estate planning, primarily by removing life insurance proceeds from your taxable estate. When structured correctly, the death benefit paid out by a policy held within an ILIT is not subject to estate tax. This can significantly reduce the tax burden on your heirs, particularly in larger estates. For blended families, ILITs can be a strategic tool to ensure that children from a previous marriage receive their intended inheritance without being impacted by estate taxes or potential disputes with a surviving spouse. The trust owns the policy, and the proceeds are distributed according to your predetermined instructions, providing an added layer of security and control. It's essential to understand that once established, an ILIT cannot be easily changed, highlighting the need for careful planning and consideration of future circumstances.

Qualified terminable interest property (QTIP) trusts provide a valuable solution for blended families grappling with the challenge of providing for both a current spouse and children from a previous marriage. These trusts allow you to provide lifetime income to your surviving spouse while ensuring that the remaining assets ultimately pass to your designated beneficiaries, often children from a previous relationship. The surviving spouse receives income generated by the trust assets, but does not have control over the principal. Upon the surviving spouse's death, the principal is distributed according to the terms of the trust, typically to children from a prior marriage. This balances the need to provide for a current spouse while safeguarding the inheritance of children from a previous relationship. This mechanism can alleviate concerns about a surviving spouse disinheriting children or favoring their own children over stepchildren.

Special needs trusts are crucial for families with children who have disabilities. These trusts are designed to provide for the beneficiary's supplemental needs without jeopardizing their eligibility for government benefits like Medicaid or Supplemental Security Income. The trust can cover expenses such as medical care, therapy, and specialized equipment that are not covered by government programs. For blended families, a special needs trust can be a vital tool to ensure that a child with disabilities receives ongoing care and support, regardless of changes in family dynamics or financial circumstances. It offers peace of mind knowing that the child's well-being is protected, regardless of the parents' future health or relationship status. Creating this type of trust requires meticulous planning and often the assistance of a specialized attorney experienced in disability law to ensure compliance with complex regulations.

Charitable remainder trusts (CRTs) offer a unique opportunity to combine philanthropic goals with estate planning benefits. By establishing a CRT, you transfer assets to a trust that provides a stream of income to designated beneficiaries, often yourself or other family members, for a specified period. After this period, the remaining assets are distributed to the designated charity. This strategy provides both an income stream for beneficiaries and a significant tax deduction at the time the trust is funded. For blended families, CRTs can be a compelling option for those who wish to leave a legacy to a charitable cause while also providing for their family members. This can be a particularly appealing option when there is a desire to support a specific charity or cause that holds significance for the family. Furthermore, CRTs can help reduce estate taxes and provide a source of income for surviving family members.

3.1 Revocable Living Trusts

A revocable living trust, often called a living trust, offers a powerful tool for managing assets during your lifetime and distributing them after your death, particularly valuable within the complex dynamics of a blended family. It allows you to retain control over your property while you're alive and dictates how it should be handled after you're gone. Unlike a will, which takes effect only after death and is subject to probate, a living trust can avoid probate altogether, saving time, expense, and potential family stress. This can be especially beneficial in blended families where navigating various relationships and competing interests can add complexity to the already challenging probate process.

A living trust involves transferring ownership of your assets, such as real estate, bank accounts, and investments, to the trust. You, as the grantor, typically serve as the trustee, managing the assets for your benefit during your lifetime. You also designate a successor trustee who will take over management and distribution of the trust assets upon your incapacitation or death. This seamless transfer of control can provide significant peace of mind, especially in situations where potential conflicts among family members are a concern. This structure ensures that your wishes are carried out efficiently and effectively, minimizing the potential for disputes. Furthermore, the privacy afforded by a living trust, avoiding the public nature of probate, is often a desirable feature for families navigating sensitive dynamics.

For blended families, a living trust can offer significant advantages in addressing the often-complex issue of inheritance. It allows you to clearly define how assets will be distributed among your spouse, children from a previous marriage, and stepchildren, reducing the possibility of misunderstandings or legal challenges. For instance, you can stipulate that your spouse receives income from the trust during their lifetime, with the remaining assets then distributed to your children. This protects your spouse's financial well-being while ensuring your children's inheritance. This level of control is difficult to achieve with a will alone.

Another benefit of a living trust is its flexibility. Because it's revocable, you can modify or even terminate it during your lifetime if your circumstances change. This adaptability is particularly relevant in blended families, where evolving relationships and changing financial situations may necessitate adjustments to your estate plan. Perhaps a new child enters the family, or the financial needs of a particular beneficiary shift. The revocable nature of the trust allows you to adapt to these changes without the need for complex legal procedures. This level of control empowers you to ensure your estate plan remains aligned with your family's current needs.

The ability of a living trust to avoid probate provides further advantages in blended families where multiple jurisdictions might be involved. If you own property in more than one state, probate proceedings would typically be required in each state, a potentially lengthy and costly process. A living trust avoids this by holding the property within the trust, which is not subject to probate in each individual state. This streamlined approach simplifies administration and can significantly reduce legal fees and administrative complexities, ultimately preserving more of your assets for your beneficiaries. The avoidance of multiple probate proceedings can be especially crucial in blended families where differing state laws could create conflicts or delays.

Moreover, a living trust can offer enhanced asset protection in certain circumstances. While not completely impenetrable, it can provide a degree of shielding from creditors and legal judgments, potentially preserving assets for your beneficiaries. This can be especially important in blended families where previous marriages or business ventures may have introduced potential liabilities. By placing assets within the trust, you create a layer of separation that can make it more difficult for creditors to reach them. This protection can be invaluable in safeguarding your family's financial future.

Finally, a living trust can offer valuable support in cases of incapacity. If you become unable to manage your affairs due to illness or injury, the successor trustee you designated can seamlessly step in and manage the trust assets according to your wishes. This avoids the need for court intervention or guardianship proceedings, providing stability and continuity for your family. In blended families, where decision-making can be complicated, this clear line of succession ensures that your financial matters are handled responsibly and according to your predetermined plan. This continuity can be crucial in minimizing stress and potential conflict during a difficult time.

By carefully considering these benefits and working with a qualified estate planning attorney, you can effectively utilize a revocable living trust to protect your assets and provide for your loved ones within the unique context of your blended family. Remember that estate planning is a dynamic process; regularly reviewing and updating your trust ensures it continues to reflect your wishes and address your family's evolving needs. The time invested in thoughtful planning now will yield invaluable peace of mind for you and your loved ones in the future.

3.2 Irrevocable Life Insurance Trusts

Irrevocable Life Insurance Trusts (ILITs) offer a powerful tool for estate planning, particularly within the complex dynamics of blended families.

An ILIT essentially holds a life insurance policy, removing its proceeds from your taxable estate. This strategy allows you to provide a substantial inheritance for your beneficiaries while mitigating potential estate tax burdens. For blended families, the control and directed distribution offered by an ILIT can be invaluable. Imagine a scenario where you want to ensure your biological children receive the death benefit from your life insurance policy, but you are also committed to providing for your current spouse. An ILIT allows you to accomplish both goals.

The irrevocable nature of the trust is a critical component. Once established, you relinquish ownership of the policy to the trust, which then becomes the owner and beneficiary. This separation of ownership is what enables the death benefit to be excluded from your estate. However, this also means you cannot make changes to the trust or the policy once it's finalized without the consent of the trustee and beneficiaries. Choosing a trustee you trust implicitly is paramount, as they will manage the trust and distribute the funds according to your wishes. This individual can be a family member, friend, or professional trustee. Careful consideration of the trustee's responsibilities and potential conflicts of interest is vital to the trust's success.

Funding the ILIT typically involves paying premiums on the life insurance policy held within the trust. You can contribute to the trust annually, and the trustee then uses these funds to pay the premiums. These contributions can be considered gifts and may be subject to gift tax rules. However, using the annual gift tax exclusion can often help minimize or eliminate any gift tax liability. Beyond the immediate estate tax benefits, an ILIT can offer significant advantages for blended families navigating complex interpersonal dynamics. By specifying how the death benefit will be distributed, you can provide clear direction and minimize the potential for disputes among family members after your passing. This clarity can be particularly important in second marriages with children from previous relationships.

Consider a scenario where a surviving spouse needs ongoing income,

while children from a prior marriage are the intended ultimate beneficiaries of the life insurance policy. The ILIT can be structured to provide income to the spouse for a specified period, with the remaining principal then distributed to the children. This arrangement balances the needs of both parties and ensures that your wishes are honored. Furthermore, ILITs offer creditor protection. The assets held within the trust are generally shielded from the creditors of both the grantor and the beneficiaries. This protection can be crucial for preserving the inheritance you intend to leave for your loved ones, especially if they face potential financial challenges.
Setting up an ILIT involves a carefully orchestrated process. It begins with selecting a trustee and beneficiaries and drafting the trust document. The life insurance policy is then transferred to the trust, and premiums are paid according to the trust's terms. Given the complexity and the irrevocable nature of the trust, working with an experienced estate planning attorney is essential. They can guide you through the process, ensuring the trust is structured correctly to meet your specific family needs and comply with all applicable laws. Careful planning and consideration of the long-term implications are key to effectively utilizing an ILIT. Don't underestimate the power of open communication within the family. Discussing your estate plan with your spouse, children, and other relevant family members can help manage expectations and prevent misunderstandings down the road. Transparency and proactive conversations can foster a smoother transition and minimize the potential for conflict during an already challenging time. Remember, an ILIT is not a one-size-fits-all solution. Its suitability depends on your individual circumstances, financial goals, and family dynamics. Other estate planning tools, such as wills, revocable living trusts, and other specialized trusts, may be used in conjunction with an ILIT to create a comprehensive estate plan. Consulting with a qualified estate planning attorney is crucial to determine the best approach for your unique situation. They can assess your needs, explain the various options, and help you design a plan that protects your assets and provides for your loved ones in the most effective way possible. Navigating the complexi-

ties of estate planning, especially within a blended family, requires careful consideration and professional guidance. By understanding the intricacies of ILITs and other estate planning tools, you can make informed decisions that secure your family's future.

3.3 Qualified Terminable Interest Trusts

Qualified terminable interest property (QTIP) trusts offer a unique blend of control and flexibility for individuals planning their estate, particularly beneficial within the context of blended families. They allow you to provide for your current spouse while simultaneously ensuring that your assets ultimately pass to your children from a previous marriage. This arrangement addresses a common concern in blended families where a surviving spouse might otherwise have complete control over the assets, potentially disinheriting the deceased spouse's children. Understanding the nuances of QTIP trusts is crucial for crafting a comprehensive estate plan that balances the needs of all family members.

A QTIP trust is established during the grantor's lifetime or upon their death through their will. The grantor designates their spouse as the sole income beneficiary for the duration of their life. This means the surviving spouse is entitled to receive all the income generated by the trust assets. This income stream can be crucial for supporting the surviving spouse's living expenses and maintaining their financial security. The grantor dictates the frequency of income distributions, whether monthly, quarterly, or annually, offering a tailored approach to the surviving spouse's financial needs.

The key feature distinguishing a QTIP trust lies in the grantor's ability to control the ultimate disposition of the assets after the surviving spouse's death. While the surviving spouse receives the income, they do not have the power to determine who inherits the trust principal. Instead, the grantor pre-determines the remainder beneficiaries, typically their children from a prior marriage. This safeguards the children's inheritance and prevents the surviving spouse from redirecting the assets to their own children or other beneficiaries.

The tax advantages of QTIP trusts are substantial. Upon the first spouse's death, the trust assets are included in their estate for estate tax purposes. However, the marital deduction allows these assets to pass to the surviving spouse tax-free, effectively deferring estate tax until the second spouse's death. This can significantly reduce the overall estate tax burden, preserving a larger portion of the family's wealth. Upon the surviving spouse's death, the trust assets are then included in their estate for tax purposes.

Establishing a QTIP trust involves careful consideration of various factors. Choosing a trustee is paramount. The trustee holds the responsibility of managing the trust assets and ensuring proper distributions to the surviving spouse. Selecting a trustworthy and competent individual or institution is essential for the effective administration of the trust and protection of the beneficiaries' interests. This individual should understand the complex nature of QTIP trusts and be capable of navigating potential legal and financial challenges.

Determining the appropriate assets to fund the QTIP trust requires a comprehensive assessment of the grantor's estate. A diverse range of assets, including real estate, stocks, bonds, and other investments, can be held within the QTIP. Careful selection of assets can help optimize the trust's performance and meet the specific financial objectives outlined by the grantor. For example, income-generating assets may be prioritized to provide a stable income stream for the surviving spouse.

Regular review and potential modifications to the QTIP trust are crucial. Life circumstances and financial situations can change over time. Adjustments may be necessary to address unforeseen events, such as a significant change in the surviving spouse's health or financial needs. Working with an experienced estate planning attorney ensures the QTIP remains aligned with the grantor's intentions and continues to serve the best interests of all beneficiaries. This ongoing management is crucial for the long-term success of the trust.

Finally, open communication with all family members involved is essential throughout the QTIP planning process. Transparency about the trust's purpose, its provisions, and the reasoning behind its establishment can help mitigate potential misunderstandings and conflicts. This open dialogue fosters a sense of shared understanding and promotes harmonious family relationships, vital aspects of effective estate planning. By addressing concerns proactively and ensuring everyone is informed, families can navigate the intricacies of blended family dynamics and build a secure financial future for all involved. A well-structured QTIP trust, combined with clear communication, can be a powerful tool for preserving family harmony and providing financial security for generations to come.

3.4 Special Needs Trusts

A Special Needs Trust (SNT) is a unique legal instrument designed to provide for the supplemental needs of a beneficiary with a disability while preserving their eligibility for government benefits like Supplemental Security Income (SSI) and Medicaid. These programs often have strict income and asset limits, and an inheritance or personal injury settlement could disqualify a beneficiary. The SNT acts as a protective barrier, holding assets for the beneficiary's benefit without impacting their means-tested benefits. This allows the trust to pay for expenses that are not covered by government programs, substantially improving the beneficiary's quality of life.

There are three primary types of SNTs: (1) Third-Party SNTs, (2) First-Party SNTs, and (3) Pooled Trusts. Understanding the distinctions between these types is critical for choosing the correct one. A Third-Party SNT is funded with assets from someone other than the beneficiary, such as a parent, grandparent, or other relative. This type of trust offers greater flexibility in terms of distributions and what happens to the remaining funds after the beneficiary's passing. The assets are not typically subject to a payback to the state upon the beneficiary's death.

In contrast, a First-Party SNT is funded with the beneficiary's own assets.

This might be from an inheritance, a personal injury settlement, or other funds belonging to the individual with the disability. While providing the same supplemental support, a crucial difference with this type of trust is the Medicaid payback provision. Upon the beneficiary's death, the state will generally seek reimbursement for Medicaid benefits paid from the remaining trust assets. This ensures that public funds are recouped, though it can limit the inheritance passed on to other family members. Careful planning and drafting are vital to minimize this payback while maximizing the benefits for the beneficiary during their lifetime.

Finally, a Pooled Trust is managed by a non-profit organization and consists of funds from multiple beneficiaries. Each beneficiary retains a separate account within the larger pool, benefiting from professional management and potentially lower administrative fees. Pooled trusts, like First-Party SNTs, are also subject to the Medicaid payback provision upon the beneficiary's death. Choosing between a First-Party SNT and a Pooled Trust often depends on the complexity of the beneficiary's needs and the family's comfort level with managing trust assets.

Drafting a Special Needs Trust requires careful attention to detail and adherence to specific legal requirements. The trust document must explicitly state that distributions are intended for supplemental needs and will not jeopardize government benefits. Vague language or overly broad distribution clauses can undermine the trust's purpose and inadvertently disqualify the beneficiary from essential programs. Choosing a trustee, the individual responsible for managing the trust assets, is another critical decision. The trustee must be someone who understands the beneficiary's needs, can manage finances responsibly, and is committed to acting in the beneficiary's best interest. This could be a family member, a professional trustee, or a corporate trustee, depending on the complexity of the trust and the family's circumstances.

Beyond the technicalities of drafting, the true power of a Special Needs Trust lies in its ability to enhance the quality of life for individuals with disabilities. The trust can fund a wide range of expenses not covered by government programs, such as specialized medical equipment, adaptive technology, therapeutic services, transportation, and even recreational activities. By addressing these unmet needs, the SNT helps the beneficiary achieve greater independence, pursue their passions, and live a fuller, more enriching life. For families navigating the complexities of caring for a loved one with a disability, the SNT offers peace of mind, knowing that their loved one's future is secure and their specific needs will be met. It's a powerful tool for ensuring that individuals with disabilities have the resources they need to thrive. Consult with a qualified estate planning attorney experienced in Special Needs Trusts to determine the best type of trust for your family's unique situation and to ensure that the trust document is properly drafted and administered. This specialized legal expertise is essential for navigating the complexities of SNTs and maximizing their benefits.

3.5 Charitable Remainder Trusts

Charitable Remainder Trusts (CRTs) offer a unique blend of philanthropic giving and financial planning, making them a valuable tool within a comprehensive estate plan, particularly for blended families. They allow you to contribute assets to a trust that eventually benefits a chosen charity while receiving income payments for a specified period. This chapter will delve into the intricacies of CRTs, exploring their different types, benefits, and considerations for blended families.

CRTs come in two primary forms: Charitable Remainder Annuity Trusts (CRATs) and Charitable Remainder Unitrusts (CRUTs). A CRAT provides a fixed annual payment to the income beneficiaries, calculated as a percentage of the initial trust assets. This fixed income stream offers predictability, making it suitable for individuals seeking a stable income supplement. Conversely, a CRUT distributes a variable annual payment based on a fixed percentage of the trust's annually revalued assets. While this can result in fluctuating income, it also offers the potential for higher payouts if the trust assets appreciate in value. Choosing between a CRAT and a CRUT depends on your individual circumstances and financial goals. Consider your risk tolerance and need for income stability when making this decision.

The benefits of incorporating a CRT into your estate plan are multifaceted. First, you receive an immediate income tax deduction for the present value of the remainder interest that will eventually go to the charity. This can significantly reduce your current tax liability. Second, the assets within the trust grow tax-deferred, potentially maximizing the eventual benefit for both the income beneficiaries and the charity. Third, CRTs can help diversify your investment portfolio and provide a stream of income secured by the trust assets. For blended families, CRTs can also serve as a neutral ground for charitable giving, fostering a sense of shared purpose and legacy.

When considering a CRT for a blended family, several important factors warrant careful consideration. Clearly defining the income beneficiaries and their respective payout periods is crucial. This might involve designating current spouses, children from previous marriages, or even grandchildren. Transparency and open communication among family members are paramount to ensure everyone understands the terms of the trust and their potential benefits. This proactive approach can minimize potential misunderstandings or conflicts down the road. Additionally, the choice of charity and the timing of the eventual charitable distribution should align with the family's values and philanthropic goals. Discussing these aspects openly within the family can strengthen bonds and create a shared legacy of giving.

Furthermore, the selection of trust assets is a critical decision. Highly appreciated assets with a low cost basis, such as real estate or stocks, are often ideal for funding a CRT. Transferring these assets into the trust allows you to avoid capital gains taxes that would otherwise be due upon their sale. However, it's essential to consider the potential impact on your overall financial plan and diversification strategy. Consulting with a financial advisor can help you determine the most suitable assets to contribute to the

CRT. This professional guidance is invaluable in ensuring the trust aligns with your broader financial objectives.

Finally, the complexities of tax laws and regulations surrounding CRTs necessitate seeking professional advice from an estate planning attorney. They can guide you through the intricate legal requirements, ensuring the trust is properly structured and administered. Moreover, an attorney can tailor the trust to the unique circumstances of your blended family, addressing specific concerns and objectives. This personalized approach is essential for maximizing the benefits of a CRT while minimizing potential pitfalls. Proper legal counsel can also help navigate the complexities of state laws, which can vary significantly, and ensure compliance with all applicable regulations.

A thoughtfully designed and implemented CRT can be a powerful tool for achieving both financial and philanthropic goals. It provides a flexible framework for managing assets, generating income, and leaving a lasting legacy. For blended families, a CRT can serve as a unifying element, fostering shared values and contributing to a common philanthropic vision. However, the intricacies of CRTs demand careful planning and professional guidance. Engaging an experienced estate planning attorney and financial advisor is essential for navigating the complexities and maximizing the benefits of this valuable estate planning tool. Remember, the long-term success of a CRT hinges on a clear understanding of its structure, benefits, and potential implications for all beneficiaries.

4 Estate Tax Considerations

Understanding the estate tax is crucial for effective estate planning, especially for blended families with complex asset structures. The federal estate tax is a tax on the transfer of property at death. It applies to the fair market value of the deceased person's gross estate, which includes all assets they owned or controlled at the time of death. This can encompass real estate, stocks, bonds, retirement accounts, life insurance benefits, and other personal property. Calculating the estate tax involves determining the gross estate, subtracting allowable deductions, and applying the applicable tax rates to the remaining taxable estate. The tax rates are progressive, meaning higher tax rates apply to larger estates.

The applicable exclusion amount plays a significant role in estate tax calculations. This is the amount that can be excluded from the gross estate before the tax is applied. The exclusion amount is adjusted annually for inflation. For deaths in 2023, the basic exclusion amount is $12.92 million per individual. This means a married couple can potentially shield up to $25.84 million from federal estate tax. However, it's important to note that portability, the ability to transfer any unused portion of a deceased spouse's exclusion to the surviving spouse, is a crucial aspect of estate tax planning. Without proper planning, a significant portion of the exclusion could be lost if the first spouse to die doesn't fully utilize it. This is particularly relevant in blended families where assets may be divided between multiple beneficiaries.

Several deductions can reduce the taxable estate, further minimizing potential estate tax liability. Marital and charitable deductions are key considerations. The unlimited marital deduction allows for the tax-free transfer of assets to a surviving spouse, US citizen. This is a valuable tool for preserving wealth within the family, especially when combined with portability. The charitable deduction allows for an unlimited deduction for assets bequeathed to qualified charitable organizations. Incorporating charitable giving into estate plans can significantly reduce the taxable estate while also supporting causes important to the family. Administrative expenses, such as funeral costs and executor fees, are also deductible, reducing the overall tax burden. Debts and mortgages owed by the decedent are deductible as well, reflecting the net value of the estate.

Beyond these deductions, several strategies exist for minimizing estate tax liability within the context of a blended family. Gifting assets during life can be a powerful tool. The annual gift tax exclusion allows individuals to gift a certain amount each year to any number of recipients without incurring gift tax. In 2023, this exclusion is $17,000 per recipient. Utilizing this annual exclusion strategically can gradually reduce the size of the taxable estate over time. Lifetime gifts, even those exceeding the annual exclusion, are sheltered by the lifetime gift and estate tax exemption, unified into a single limit. While these gifts may use a portion of the lifetime exemption, they remove future appreciation of those assets from the taxable estate.

Establishing trusts can be another effective strategy. Certain trusts, such as irrevocable life insurance trusts (ILITs), can hold life insurance policies outside of the estate, preventing the death benefit from being included in the gross estate. This is particularly useful for larger estates where life insurance proceeds could significantly impact the estate tax calculation. Grantor retained annuity trusts (GRATs) and qualified personal residence trusts (QPRTs) are more sophisticated strategies that can freeze the value of assets for estate tax purposes, effectively transferring future appreciation to beneficiaries without incurring immediate gift tax. However, these strategies require careful planning and professional advice due to their complexities. They are particularly relevant when dealing with significant assets like family businesses or valuable real estate. Understanding the nuances of these strategies, including the potential impact of interest rates and life expectancies, is crucial for maximizing their effectiveness.

Furthermore, careful consideration of beneficiary designations is essential. Properly designating beneficiaries on retirement accounts and life insurance policies ensures that assets pass directly to the intended recipients outside of probate, potentially avoiding estate tax. This can be particularly important in blended families where multiple sets of children or stepchildren are involved. Reviewing and updating beneficiary designations regularly is vital to reflect changing family circumstances and ensure that assets are distributed according to the decedent's wishes. This can help prevent unintended consequences and minimize potential conflicts among beneficiaries. Furthermore, open communication within the family about estate plans can alleviate uncertainty and foster a greater sense of understanding among all parties involved. This proactive approach can significantly contribute to a smoother transition and preservation of family relationships during a challenging time.

4.1 Calculating the Estate Tax

Understanding how the estate tax is calculated is crucial for effective estate planning, especially in blended families where the complexities of multiple marriages and sets of heirs can significantly impact the final tax burden. The estate tax, a federal tax levied on the transfer of property at death, applies only to estates exceeding a certain threshold, a figure adjusted annually for inflation. This threshold, known as the applicable exclusion amount, represents the value of assets that can be transferred tax-free. Any estate value above this amount is potentially subject to estate tax, calculated using a graduated tax rate system. These rates can range from 18% to 40% in 2023, depending on the size of the taxable estate. It's vital to remember that the estate tax calculation hinges on the net value of the estate, meaning the total value of all assets minus allowable deductions.

Determining the gross estate value is the first step in the calculation. This involves meticulously identifying and valuing all assets owned at the time of death. These assets can encompass a wide range, from tangible property like real estate, vehicles, and personal belongings to intangible assets such as stocks, bonds, retirement accounts, and business interests. Even assets held jointly with another person, such as a jointly owned bank account or property held as tenants in common, may be partially or wholly included in the gross estate, depending on the ownership structure and applicable state laws. Life insurance proceeds, though often considered non-probate assets, are typically included in the gross estate if the decedent owned the policy or retained any incident of ownership. Accurately valuing these diverse assets is critical, as undervaluation can lead to penalties and complications later on. Often, professional appraisers are employed to determine the fair market value of complex assets like real estate or business interests.

Once the gross estate is established, certain deductions can be subtracted to arrive at the taxable estate. These deductions play a vital role in minimizing the ultimate tax liability. Allowable deductions include funeral expenses, administrative costs associated with settling the estate, outstanding debts, and certain state and foreign death taxes. A significant deduction available is the marital deduction, which allows for an unlimited transfer of assets to a surviving spouse free from estate tax. This deduction is particularly relevant in blended families where careful planning can ensure its optimal use, potentially reducing the taxable estate significantly. Charitable contributions made through the estate are also deductible, further diminishing the taxable base.

Understanding how the applicable exclusion amount functions is paramount. This amount, which has historically fluctuated due to legislative changes, provides a crucial shield against estate tax. For 2023, the applicable exclusion amount is notably high, allowing a considerable value of assets to be passed down tax-free. However, it's essential to understand that this exclusion amount is portable between spouses. This portability feature allows a surviving spouse to use any unused portion of their deceased spouse's exclusion, effectively doubling the tax-free threshold for the surviving spouse's estate. This can be especially valuable in blended families where assets may be unevenly distributed between spouses.

Navigating the complexities of estate tax calculations requires careful consideration of all assets, deductions, and the applicable exclusion amount. For blended families, these calculations can become even more intricate due to the potential involvement of multiple sets of beneficiaries and varied asset ownership structures. Engaging with a qualified estate planning attorney is highly recommended. They can provide personalized guidance tailored to your specific family circumstances, ensuring that your estate plan minimizes potential tax liabilities and aligns with your long-term financial goals. This professional advice can be instrumental in navigating the intricacies of estate tax law and maximizing the benefits of available exemptions and deductions.

Effective estate planning requires proactive consideration of potential future tax implications. While the current estate tax exclusion amount is substantial, future legislative changes could significantly alter this landscape. It's wise to structure your estate plan with flexibility, anticipating potential shifts in tax law. Strategies such as gifting assets during your lifetime can be a powerful tool in managing your taxable estate while also benefiting your loved ones. Such gifts, made within the annual gift tax exclusion limits, can progressively reduce the size of your estate and consequently lower the potential estate tax burden. Consulting with a financial advisor can provide valuable insights into strategies for strategically gifting assets while minimizing potential gift tax implications.

The effective use of trusts can be another crucial element in mitigating estate taxes, especially for blended families. Different types of trusts, such as irrevocable life insurance trusts (ILITs) or Qualified Terminable Interest Property (QTIP) trusts, can offer significant tax advantages while also providing control over how assets are distributed. An ILIT, for example, can hold life insurance policies outside of the estate, thereby excluding the proceeds from estate tax calculations. QTIP trusts allow assets to be transferred to a surviving spouse while ensuring that the remainder ultimately passes to designated beneficiaries, such as children from a previous marriage. Understanding the specific benefits and limitations of various trust structures is essential for crafting a comprehensive and tax-efficient estate plan. Working with an experienced estate planning attorney can provide clarity on the best trust options for your unique family situation. They can guide you in selecting the most appropriate tools to achieve your estate planning objectives while minimizing tax liabilities. Furthermore, they can assist in drafting trust documents that are legally sound and tailored to your specific needs.

4.2 Exemptions and Deductions

Navigating the complexities of estate tax can be a daunting task, especially for blended families. Understanding available exemptions and deductions is crucial for minimizing potential tax burdens and ensuring a smooth transfer of wealth. The applicable exclusion amount, which is the value of an estate exempt from federal estate tax, changes periodically due to inflation adjustments. This exclusion, a substantial amount, effectively shields a significant portion of most estates from federal estate tax. However, for estates exceeding this threshold, careful planning becomes essential to mitigate tax liabilities.

Beyond the applicable exclusion amount, several key deductions can further reduce the taxable estate. The marital deduction, a powerful tool, allows for an unlimited transfer of assets between spouses during life or at death, free from federal estate tax. This deduction is particularly relevant for blended families, where spouses may have children from previous relationships. By utilizing the marital deduction, couples can maximize the tax benefits available to them and ensure that assets are preserved for their surviving spouse and, ultimately, their intended beneficiaries.

Another significant deduction is the charitable deduction. This allows for an unlimited deduction for assets bequeathed to qualified charitable organizations. For philanthropically inclined individuals in blended families, this deduction offers a way to support their chosen causes while simultaneously reducing their taxable estate. The interplay of the marital and charitable deductions can be a powerful strategy in minimizing estate tax liability, especially for larger estates. It's important to note that while these deductions offer substantial tax benefits, they also require careful consideration of the family's overall financial goals and philanthropic intentions. Beyond these primary deductions, certain expenses associated with the administration of the estate can also be deducted. These include executor fees, attorney fees, and appraisal costs. While individually these deductions may seem relatively small, they can collectively contribute to a noticeable reduction in the taxable estate. Accurate record-keeping is essential to substantiate these deductions during the estate tax filing process. Meticulous documentation of all expenses related to the estate administration is paramount to ensure that all legitimate deductions are claimed and the tax liability is minimized.

Understanding the interplay of the applicable exclusion amount and these deductions is paramount for effective estate tax planning in blended families. For example, a surviving spouse can utilize the deceased spouse's unused applicable exclusion amount, effectively doubling the amount shielded from estate tax. This portability provision, enacted relatively recently, provides a significant benefit for married couples, particularly in second marriages where individuals may have substantial assets accumulated prior to their current union. Careful coordination of estate planning documents, including wills and trusts, is essential to leverage the portability provision effectively.

However, the landscape of estate tax is subject to change, influenced by legislative updates and evolving economic conditions. It is crucial to stay informed about potential changes to estate tax laws, as these could significantly impact estate planning strategies. Staying up-to-date on current tax laws and regulations is essential for making informed decisions and adapting plans as needed. Consulting with a qualified estate planning attorney is highly recommended to navigate the complexities of estate tax and ensure that your plan is current and effective.

In blended families, the nuances of estate tax planning become even more intricate. The presence of children from prior relationships can introduce complexities regarding inheritance distribution and potential tax implications. Open communication within the family regarding estate planning decisions is crucial to minimize potential conflicts and ensure a smooth transition of assets. Transparency and dialogue among family members can help to clarify expectations, address concerns, and foster a sense of shared understanding. This can be invaluable in preventing misunderstandings and disputes that can arise after a loved one's passing.

Properly structured trusts can also be instrumental in minimizing estate tax liability in blended families. For example, a Qualified Terminable Interest Property (QTIP) trust allows a surviving spouse to receive income from trust assets while ensuring that the remaining principal ultimately passes to the grantor's children from a previous relationship. This can be a valuable tool for balancing the needs of a surviving spouse with the desire to provide for children from a prior marriage. QTIP trusts offer a degree of control over the ultimate disposition of assets, while still providing for the surviving spouse's financial well-being.

Ultimately, effective estate tax planning for blended families requires a comprehensive approach that considers the unique dynamics of each family's situation. Seeking professional guidance from an experienced estate planning attorney and a qualified financial advisor is essential to develop a tailored plan that addresses individual needs and goals, minimizing potential tax liabilities and ensuring a smooth transfer of wealth to future generations. This collaborative approach ensures that all aspects of the family's financial situation are considered, leading to a more robust and effective estate plan.

4.3 Minimizing Estate Tax Liability

Minimizing estate tax liability is a crucial aspect of estate planning, particularly for blended families with complex asset structures and multiple beneficiaries. One primary strategy involves leveraging the applicable estate tax exemption. Currently, there's a substantial federal estate tax exemption, and many states also have their own exemptions or no estate tax at all. Understanding these exemptions and how they can be utilized is essential. For example, married couples can effectively double their federal exemption through portability, allowing the surviving spouse to use any unused portion of the deceased spouse's exemption. This can significantly reduce or eliminate estate tax liability for many families. However, state estate tax laws can differ significantly, and careful consideration must be given to residency and domicile rules.

Beyond exemptions, effectively utilizing deductions can further mitigate estate tax burdens. Charitable bequests, for example, are deductible from the gross estate. This means that assets left to qualified charitable organizations are not subject to estate tax. Families can establish charitable remainder trusts (CRTs) or charitable lead trusts (CLTs) to provide income for beneficiaries while ultimately benefiting a chosen charity and reducing the taxable estate. Another significant deduction is the marital deduction, which allows for unlimited tax-free transfers of assets between spouses. This is particularly relevant for blended families where assets may need to be transferred between spouses to equalize inheritances or provide for a surviving spouse. Properly structuring these transfers, potentially through trusts, is crucial to ensure the deduction is applied correctly while also addressing the specific needs and concerns of the blended family structure.

Gifting assets during life can be another powerful tool for reducing estate tax liability. The annual gift tax exclusion allows individuals to gift a certain amount each year to any number of recipients without incurring gift tax. This can be used strategically to gradually reduce the size of the taxable estate over time. Additionally, lifetime gifts, even those exceeding the annual exclusion, can utilize the lifetime gift tax exemption, further reducing the eventual taxable estate. For blended families, gifting can be a particularly useful strategy for equalizing inheritances among children from different marriages or providing for specific needs, such as education expenses. It is important, however, to carefully consider the implications of gifting on the donor's financial security and the potential impact on family dynamics.

Strategic use of trusts can play a significant role in minimizing estate taxes. Irrevocable Life Insurance Trusts (ILITs), for instance, can remove life insurance proceeds from the taxable estate, provided the trust is structured correctly. This is particularly important for high-net-worth individuals where life insurance benefits constitute a substantial portion of their estate. Similarly, Grantor Retained Annuity Trusts (GRATs) and Qualified Personal Residence Trusts (QPRTs) can be effective tools for transferring assets while minimizing gift and estate tax implications. These trusts allow for the transfer of appreciating assets, such as real estate or business interests, while freezing the value for estate tax purposes. This can be particularly beneficial in a low-interest-rate environment. For blended families, trusts can also provide a mechanism for controlling the distribution of assets to different beneficiaries, ensuring that each branch of the family is treated equitably according to the decedent's wishes.

Estate planning for blended families often involves complex considerations related to the varying needs and relationships within the family structure. Beyond tax minimization, preserving family harmony is paramount. Open communication and transparency throughout the estate planning process are crucial. Family meetings can provide a forum for discussing estate planning goals and addressing any concerns or questions. Involving a qualified estate planning attorney experienced in working with blended families is highly recommended. They can provide objective advice, facilitate communication, and draft legally sound documents that reflect the family's unique circumstances. They can also help navigate the intricate web of estate tax laws, ensuring that the chosen strategies are effective and compliant.

Finally, regular review and updates to estate plans are essential. Tax laws, family circumstances, and financial situations can change over time, impacting the effectiveness of existing plans. Regular reviews, ideally with the estate planning attorney, allow for adjustments and ensure the plan continues to align with the family's goals and evolving needs. This ongoing process of review and revision is particularly important for blended families, as changes in family dynamics can significantly affect estate distribution plans. By staying proactive and informed, families can minimize potential conflicts and ensure that their estate plan remains a source of security and stability for all beneficiaries.

5 Gift Tax Implications

Understanding the intricacies of gift tax is crucial for effective estate planning, particularly within the context of blended families. While often overlooked, gifting assets during your lifetime can be a powerful tool for minimizing your eventual estate tax burden and directing your wealth precisely as you intend. It allows you to witness the benefits of your generosity and provides a degree of control that extends beyond the provisions of a will. This control can be especially valuable in blended family situations, where managing the distribution of assets among multiple sets of heirs can be complex.

A key component of gift tax law revolves around the annual gift tax exclusion. For 2023, this exclusion allows you to gift up to $17,000 per recipient without incurring any gift tax liability or even needing to file a gift tax return. This exclusion applies to each individual recipient, meaning you could gift $17,000 to each of your children, stepchildren, and any other individuals you choose, each year, without any gift tax consequences. This annual exclusion is indexed for inflation and may adjust in future years. Understanding and utilizing this annual exclusion can significantly reduce the size of your taxable estate over time, especially if you begin gifting strategically early in your life. Imagine a blended family with two children from a previous marriage and three stepchildren. Utilizing the annual exclusion effectively allows for a considerable amount of tax-free gifting each year.

Beyond the annual exclusion lies the lifetime gift tax exemption. This exemption, a substantial amount set by the IRS, allows you to gift a significant sum over the course of your lifetime without triggering gift tax. For 2023, this exemption is set at $12.92 million per individual. This means that any gifts exceeding the annual exclusion are deducted from your lifetime exemption amount. Once this exemption is exhausted, any further gifts above the annual exclusion amount become subject to gift tax. This exemption, when used in conjunction with the annual exclusion, provides a considerable opportunity to transfer wealth tax-free. For high-net-worth individuals in blended families, this can be a crucial element in preserving assets for intended beneficiaries while minimizing the impact of estate taxes.

Effective utilization of the lifetime gift tax exemption requires careful planning. Consider the potential appreciation of gifted assets. If you gift an asset that is expected to increase significantly in value, the future appreciation will not be included in your taxable estate. This can be a particularly advantageous strategy for assets like real estate or stocks. For example, gifting a portion of a vacation home to your children and stepchildren now, while its value is still relatively low, can remove future appreciation from your estate, minimizing potential estate tax liability down the line.

However, the gift tax regulations are complex and include certain nuances. Gifts to a spouse who is a U.S. citizen are generally unlimited and not subject to gift tax. However, gifts to a non-citizen spouse are subject to a different set of rules with a higher annual exclusion limit, which requires careful consideration and often professional advice. In the context of blended families, where prior marriages and international relationships might be a factor, understanding these nuances is particularly important.

Another area requiring careful navigation in the realm of gift tax is the treatment of tuition and medical expenses. Direct payments made to educational institutions for tuition or to medical providers for qualified medical expenses on behalf of any individual are not considered taxable gifts, regardless of the amount. This provides another avenue for tax-advantaged giving, particularly helpful for blended families looking to contribute to the education or healthcare costs of their children and stepchildren without impacting their lifetime gift tax exemption or annual exclusion amounts. These direct payments provide a valuable tool for supporting family members while maintaining control over the use of funds. Gifting can be a powerful tool in estate planning, particularly for blended families. By understanding and strategically employing the annual gift tax exclusion and lifetime gift tax exemption, individuals can significantly reduce their taxable estate, provide for their loved ones, and facilitate a smoother transfer of wealth. However, the complexities of gift tax law, particularly within the framework of blended families, necessitate careful consideration and often the guidance of a qualified estate planning professional. They can help tailor a gifting strategy specific to your family's circumstances, ensuring that your assets are distributed according to your wishes while minimizing potential tax liabilities. By working with a professional, you can confidently navigate the intricacies of gift tax and integrate it into a comprehensive estate plan that reflects your unique family dynamics and financial goals. Ultimately, a well-structured gifting strategy provides not only financial benefits but also peace of mind, knowing that you have taken proactive steps to secure your family's future.

5.1 Annual Gift Tax Exclusion

Leveraging the annual gift tax exclusion is a powerful tool in estate planning, especially for blended families. This exclusion allows you to gift a certain amount of money each year to as many individuals as you like, free from federal gift tax. Understanding and strategically utilizing this exclusion can significantly reduce your taxable estate over time, preserving more of your wealth for your intended beneficiaries. For 2023, the annual exclusion is set at $17,000 per recipient. This means you can gift up to $17,000 to each of your children, stepchildren, or anyone else, without incurring any gift tax liability. For married couples, this amount effectively doubles. Utilizing what is known as gift splitting, a married couple can combine their annual exclusions and gift up to $34,000 per recipient tax-free.

Consider the long-term impact. Even seemingly small annual gifts can accumulate significantly over time. If you consistently gift the maximum exclusion amount to multiple beneficiaries each year, the cumulative effect on your taxable estate can be substantial. Imagine gifting $17,000 each year for ten years to just one beneficiary. That's $170,000 removed from your estate, potentially saving thousands in estate taxes down the line. Now, multiply that by multiple beneficiaries – children, stepchildren, grandchildren – and the impact becomes even more pronounced. This strategy is particularly valuable for blended families, where ensuring equitable distribution of assets across multiple family branches can be complex.

The annual gift tax exclusion applies to a wide range of assets, not just cash. You can gift stocks, bonds, real estate, or even interests in a family business. The value of the gift is determined at the time of the transfer. For example, if you gift stock worth $17,000 today, and it appreciates to $25,000 next year, only the original $17,000 counts towards your annual exclusion. Any future appreciation is not subject to gift tax. This aspect of the exclusion can be particularly advantageous when gifting assets with growth potential.

Keep meticulous records. While these gifts are tax-free, maintaining comprehensive records is crucial. Document each gift, including the date, recipient, asset transferred, and its fair market value. These records will be invaluable in case of an audit or if questions arise about your estate's value. Proper documentation also simplifies the process for your heirs and executors, providing clarity and minimizing potential disputes. This meticulous record-keeping becomes even more critical in blended families, where the intricacies of relationships and asset distribution can easily lead to misunderstandings.

Beyond the direct financial benefits, using the annual gift tax exclusion offers additional advantages. Gifting assets while you are still alive allows you to witness the positive impact on your beneficiaries. It can be a powerful way to provide financial support for education, a down payment on a house, or the start of a business. Seeing your loved ones benefit from your generosity can be deeply rewarding. Furthermore, strategically using these gifts can help avoid potential family conflicts down the line, particularly in blended families with complex dynamics. Open communication with all parties involved about gifting strategies can foster transparency and build trust.

Coordinate with your overall estate plan. While the annual gift tax exclusion is a valuable tool, it's just one piece of the puzzle. Integrate your gifting strategy with your broader estate plan, considering your will, trusts, and other estate planning documents. This integrated approach ensures that your assets are distributed according to your wishes and that you maximize the benefits of available tax advantages. For example, combining annual exclusion gifts with the establishment of trusts for minor children or grandchildren can provide both tax benefits and long-term asset protection. This holistic perspective is particularly important for blended families, ensuring that all beneficiaries are treated fairly and that your estate plan reflects the complexities of your family structure.

Remember, while the annual gift tax exclusion offers significant advantages, it's essential to seek professional advice. Estate planning, especially for blended families, can be intricate, involving various legal and tax considerations. Consulting with an experienced estate planning attorney and a financial advisor will ensure that your gifting strategies align with your overall financial goals and comply with current tax laws. They can provide personalized guidance tailored to your unique family situation and help you navigate the complexities of blended family dynamics. Their expertise will be invaluable in crafting a comprehensive plan that protects your assets and ensures your legacy is preserved according to your wishes.

5.2 Lifetime Gift Tax Exemption

The lifetime gift tax exemption allows you to transfer a substantial amount of wealth during your life without incurring federal gift tax. Understanding this powerful tool is crucial for effective estate planning, especially in the context of blended families. This exemption, a significant figure adjusted annually for inflation, applies to the total value of gifts you make throughout your life. It's important to distinguish it from the annual gift tax exclusion, which allows for smaller, tax-free gifts each year to any number of recipients. While the annual exclusion chips away at your overall estate, the lifetime exemption provides a substantial shield against gift tax liability on larger transfers, such as gifting a down payment on a house to a child or contributing to a grandchild's 529 education plan. By utilizing this exemption strategically, you can significantly reduce the size of your taxable estate, potentially minimizing or eliminating estate tax upon your death.

For 2023, the lifetime gift and estate tax exemption stands at $12.92 million per individual. This means a married couple can potentially shield over $25 million from gift and estate taxes. This substantial exemption offers significant planning opportunities, particularly for blended families seeking to provide for children from previous relationships while ensuring fairness and minimizing potential conflict. Consider a scenario where you wish to provide financial assistance to your child from a previous marriage without impacting your current spouse's inheritance. Utilizing your lifetime gift tax exemption to make a substantial gift, perhaps towards a business venture or real estate purchase, can accomplish this goal without depleting assets intended for your spouse.

However, the lifetime gift tax exemption is not without its nuances. Gifts that qualify for the annual exclusion do not count against your lifetime exemption. This means you can make annual gifts up to the exclusion limit ($17,000 per recipient in 2023) without eroding your lifetime exemption amount. This allows for ongoing, tax-free gifting strategies, alongside larger transfers that leverage the lifetime exemption. Imagine gifting the annual exclusion amount to each of your children and stepchildren every year. This consistent gifting strategy not only benefits your family members but also gradually reduces the size of your taxable estate over time. Coupled with strategic use of the lifetime exemption for larger transfers, such as contributing to a trust, you can create a comprehensive plan that minimizes future tax liabilities.

While using the lifetime exemption may seem straightforward, several complexities warrant careful consideration. Gifts of future interests, meaning gifts where the recipient doesn't have immediate access or control, don't qualify for the annual exclusion. These gifts, however, do count against your lifetime exemption. This distinction becomes particularly important when considering trusts. For instance, contributing to an irrevocable trust for a beneficiary may utilize a portion of your lifetime exemption, even if the beneficiary doesn't immediately receive the funds. Understanding this distinction is essential for making informed decisions and optimizing the use of your exemption.

Gifting assets that are expected to appreciate significantly in value presents another layer of complexity. The value of the gift for tax purposes is generally its fair market value at the time of the gift. If the asset appreciates substantially after the gift, that appreciation escapes gift and estate tax. This can be a powerful tool for transferring wealth efficiently to the next generation. Consider gifting shares in a promising startup company to your children. If the company's value skyrockets in the future, that growth occurs outside of your taxable estate, maximizing the benefit of the gift.

Furthermore, it's crucial to document all gifts meticulously. Maintaining thorough records of the gift's value, the date it was given, and the recipient is essential for accurate tax reporting and can prevent future disputes. This meticulous record-keeping is especially important in blended families, where clear documentation can help avoid misunderstandings and maintain harmony among family members. Imagine a situation where a dispute arises regarding past gifts after your passing. Detailed records can provide clarity and prevent prolonged legal battles, protecting your family from unnecessary stress and expense.

Finally, remember that tax laws are subject to change. The lifetime gift tax exemption, while currently substantial, could be reduced by future legislation. Staying informed about potential changes and consulting with a qualified estate planning attorney is crucial for adapting your strategies and ensuring your plan remains effective. This proactive approach becomes even more important for blended families, as changes in tax law can have significant implications for how assets are distributed and can potentially exacerbate existing family dynamics. Working with an experienced attorney can help you navigate these complexities and ensure your estate plan reflects your wishes, regardless of future legislative changes. They can provide tailored guidance based on your specific family structure and financial situation, creating a robust plan that protects your loved ones and minimizes potential tax liabilities.

6 Protecting Assets for Children

Safeguarding a child's inheritance requires careful planning, especially within the complex dynamics of a blended family. Consider the various stages of a child's life and the potential challenges they may face. This proactive approach can help ensure their financial well-being throughout their lives. Implementing these strategies early allows for adjustments as circumstances change, mitigating potential future disputes and providing a stable financial foundation for your children.

Start with guardianship designations. A will should clearly name guardians for minor children in the event of both parents' deaths. This critical decision ensures that your children are cared for by individuals you trust and who share your values. Consider not only their ability to provide a loving home but also their financial stability and overall suitability for raising your children. Regularly review and update these designations as family circumstances evolve.

Custodial accounts, under the Uniform Transfers to Minors Act (UTMA) or the Uniform Gifts to Minors Act (UGMA), offer a simple way to manage assets for minors. These accounts allow assets to be held for the benefit of the child until they reach the age of majority, at which point they gain full control. While straightforward to establish, custodial accounts offer limited control over how the assets are ultimately used. Furthermore, they become the child's property outright, potentially exposing them to creditors or legal claims.

Trusts for minor children provide greater flexibility and protection. They allow you to dictate how and when assets are distributed, even after the child reaches adulthood. You can specify conditions for distributions, such as educational milestones or reaching a certain age, ensuring responsible use of the funds. Furthermore, assets held in trust are generally protected from creditors and the potential financial fallout of a future divorce. Different types of trusts can be tailored to meet specific needs and family situations.

Education planning is another crucial element of securing a child's future. 529 plans offer tax-advantaged savings for qualified education expenses. These plans allow investments to grow tax-deferred, and withdrawals are tax-free when used for eligible expenses, including tuition, fees, and room and board. Consider establishing separate 529 plans for each child to ensure dedicated funds for their individual educational pursuits.

Protecting an inheritance from creditors and future divorce proceedings is equally important. Trusts, as mentioned earlier, offer significant protection. Assets held in trust are generally not considered marital property in a divorce and are typically shielded from creditors. Prenuptial agreements can also play a vital role in protecting inherited assets for children by clearly defining separate property and limiting spousal claims. Consider incorporating spendthrift provisions within trusts to further safeguard assets from irresponsible spending or creditor claims.

Life insurance can provide a crucial safety net. The death benefit can replace lost income, ensuring the continuation of financial support for your children. Life insurance proceeds can be used to fund trusts, pay off debts, or cover future expenses, protecting the inheritance you intend to leave behind. Review your life insurance coverage regularly to ensure it aligns with your family's evolving needs.

Clear communication with all family members, especially in blended families, is essential. Openly discussing your estate plan can minimize misunderstandings and potential conflicts down the road. Transparency builds

trust and helps everyone understand their roles and responsibilities, promoting a smoother transition and preserving family harmony. While potentially uncomfortable, these conversations are crucial for managing expectations and mitigating future disputes.
Regularly review and update your estate plan. Life changes, such as births, deaths, marriages, and divorces, necessitate adjustments to your plan. Reviewing your plan at least annually or after any significant life event ensures it remains current and reflects your wishes. Consult with an estate planning attorney to address any necessary revisions and ensure your plan remains legally sound.
Finally, consider professional guidance. An experienced estate planning attorney can provide tailored advice based on your unique family situation. They can help navigate complex legal and tax implications, ensuring your assets are protected and distributed according to your wishes. A financial advisor can assist with investment strategies and ensure your estate plan aligns with your overall financial goals. Working with these professionals can provide peace of mind knowing that your children's future is secure. Remember, estate planning is not a one-time event but an ongoing process.

6.1 Guardianship Designations

Selecting a guardian for your children is arguably one of the most crucial decisions you'll make in your estate plan, especially within the complex dynamics of a blended family. This designation determines who will assume the responsibility of caring for your minor children in the event of your incapacitation or death. It's a decision laden with emotional weight and legal ramifications, demanding careful consideration that goes beyond simple familial ties. Choosing the right guardian requires a thorough assessment of various factors, always prioritizing the best interests of your children above all else. This isn't just about legal paperwork; it's about ensuring your children's well-being, security, and future in the most vulnerable of circumstances.

Consider the practicalities of daily life. Think about the potential guardian's lifestyle, living arrangements, and overall stability. Do they have the financial resources to support your children adequately? Do they live in a stable and safe environment? What is their parenting philosophy? These questions delve into the nitty-gritty of childcare, examining the everyday realities that will shape your children's lives. A comfortable home and financial security are important, but so are the less tangible aspects of upbringing, such as emotional support, discipline, and the overall environment a potential guardian provides. A loving home with limited resources might be preferable to a financially secure but emotionally detached environment.

Explore the emotional connection between the potential guardian and your children. A strong, pre-existing bond can ease the transition during a difficult time, providing a sense of familiarity and comfort. This existing relationship can be invaluable, offering emotional stability and continuity in the face of upheaval. Consider how the potential guardian interacts with your children now. Do they show genuine care and affection? Are they involved in your children's lives, attending school events, sharing holidays, or simply spending quality time together? These observations offer insights into the depth and quality of their existing relationship, helping you gauge the potential for a nurturing and supportive environment in the future.

Evaluate the potential guardian's willingness and ability to take on this significant responsibility. Guardianship isn't a task to be undertaken lightly. It requires a deep commitment of time, energy, and emotional resources. Have open and honest conversations with potential guardians. Discuss the practicalities of caring for your children, including their education, healthcare, and emotional well-being. Ensure they understand the legal and financial implications of guardianship, and that they are truly prepared to embrace this role wholeheartedly. This isn't merely a legal formality; it's a profound commitment to nurturing and protecting your children's future.

Think beyond immediate family members. While grandparents or other relatives might seem like the natural choice, they might not always be the most suitable. Age, health, or other personal circumstances can impact their ability to provide long-term care. Explore the option of close friends or trusted mentors who share your values and parenting philosophy. These individuals might offer a more stable and suitable environment for your children, even if they aren't blood relatives. The most crucial factor is identifying someone who can provide a loving, supportive, and stable home, regardless of their familial connection.

Consider the dynamics of your blended family. If your children have different biological parents, choosing a guardian from one side of the family could create conflict or complicate legal proceedings. In such situations, appointing a neutral third party, like a close family friend or professional guardian, might be a more appropriate solution. This approach can minimize potential disputes and ensure that the focus remains solely on your children's best interests, rather than becoming entangled in family politics.

Clearly document your guardianship designation in your will. This legal document formalizes your choice and provides clear instructions for the court. It should include the full name and contact information of your chosen guardian, as well as any contingent guardians in case your primary choice is unable or unwilling to serve. Precise and unambiguous language is essential to prevent misunderstandings or legal challenges down the road. This documentation is your voice, ensuring your wishes are respected and your children's future is secured.

Regularly review and update your guardianship designation. Life circumstances change, and what was suitable a few years ago might no longer be the best option. As your children grow, their needs evolve, and your family dynamics might shift. Revisit your guardianship designation periodically, ensuring it still aligns with your current circumstances and reflects your children's best interests. This ongoing review demonstrates your commitment to their well-being, adapting to life's changes to provide them with the most appropriate care and support.

Choosing a guardian for your children is a profound responsibility, demanding careful consideration and thoughtful planning. By prioritizing your children's best interests and engaging in open communication, you can create a plan that provides security and stability for their future, regardless of the complexities of your blended family structure. This decision isn't just about legal documents; it's about love, protection, and ensuring your children are cared for by someone who truly has their hearts at heart.

6.2 Custodial Accounts

Custodial accounts offer a straightforward way to manage assets for minors without the complexities of a full-fledged trust. They are created under the Uniform Transfers to Minors Act (UTMA) or its predecessor, the Uniform Gifts to Minors Act (UGMA), and allow an adult custodian to manage funds for a child's benefit until they reach the age of majority, which varies by state but is typically 18 or 21. These accounts provide a simple and cost-effective solution for smaller gifts or inheritances, offering immediate availability of the funds for the child's needs. While the custodian controls the assets, they are legally obligated to use them solely for the minor's benefit, encompassing expenses like education, healthcare, and general support.

Consider, for instance, a stepfather wanting to contribute to his stepdaughter's college fund. Establishing a custodial account allows him to earmark those funds specifically for her education while retaining control until she reaches adulthood. This offers an alternative to directly gifting the money, ensuring its intended use and preventing potential misuse. He can contribute regularly to the account, making it a convenient vehicle for ongoing savings. It's important to note that while custodial accounts are relatively easy to set up and administer, they offer limited flexibility compared to trusts.

One key difference lies in the transfer of control. Once the child reaches the age of majority, they gain full and immediate access to the funds. This can be a concern if the child is not yet financially responsible or if there are concerns about potential influence from the other parent. Imagine a situation where a custodial account is established by a grandparent for a grandchild whose parent has a history of financial mismanagement. Upon reaching majority, the child gains access to the funds, which could then be subject to influence or even appropriation by the parent. This potential vulnerability underscores the importance of carefully considering the child's maturity and the family dynamics before opting for a custodial account.

Another limitation of custodial accounts pertains to asset protection. Assets held in a custodial account are considered the child's property for legal purposes. This means they could be exposed to creditors or legal judgments against the child. In the context of a blended family, this can be particularly relevant if the child is involved in activities that carry a risk of liability, such as driving a car. If the child were to be involved in an accident and found liable for damages, the assets in the custodial account could be seized to satisfy the judgment. This potential exposure contrasts sharply with the asset protection offered by certain types of trusts, which can shield assets from creditors.

Furthermore, custodial accounts offer less control over how the funds are utilized once the child reaches majority. Unlike trusts, which can stipulate specific uses and disbursement schedules, custodial accounts offer no such mechanisms. A parent might, for instance, wish to ensure that inherited funds are primarily used for education and not frivolous spending. While they can certainly express their wishes to the child, they have no legal recourse to enforce them once the child gains control of the account. This lack of control can be a significant drawback, particularly in situations where there are concerns about the child's financial judgment or potential external pressures.

Choosing between a custodial account and a trust for a minor in a blended family requires careful consideration of the specific circumstances. For smaller sums and situations where the family dynamic is stable and the child is expected to manage finances responsibly, a custodial account may be a suitable option. However, for larger inheritances or when more control and protection are desired, establishing a trust offers greater flexibility and security. Trusts allow for ongoing management of assets beyond the age of majority, provide greater creditor protection, and can be tailored to address specific family circumstances. They also offer more options for tax planning and can help avoid probate, simplifying the process of asset transfer. The best approach often involves consulting with an experienced estate planning attorney who can assess the individual needs of the blended family and recommend the most appropriate strategy. This ensures that the chosen method aligns with the family's long-term financial goals and protects the interests of all involved. A well-crafted estate plan can provide peace of mind and help preserve family harmony for years to come. Remember, the right approach will depend on the unique circumstances of your family, the size and nature of the assets involved, and your long-term objectives.

6.3 Trusts for Minor Children

Safeguarding a child's financial future is paramount, particularly within the complex dynamics of a blended family. Trusts designed specifically for minors offer a potent tool to ensure that assets are managed responsibly and distributed according to your wishes, even after you're gone. Unlike outright gifts or custodial accounts, trusts provide a structured approach, offering flexibility and control that adapts to the child's evolving needs. This level of oversight becomes even more critical in blended families, where varying familial relationships can create unique financial considerations. Think of it as a safety net, meticulously crafted to catch your child's inheritance and protect it from potential misuse or mismanagement.

A significant advantage of trusts for minors is their ability to bypass the probate process. Probate, the often lengthy and public court procedure for validating wills and distributing assets, can be both costly and time-consuming. By placing assets within a trust, you create a direct path for their transfer to your beneficiaries, avoiding the delays and expenses associated with probate court. This streamlined approach ensures that your child's inheritance is readily accessible when needed, rather than tied up in legal proceedings. Furthermore, the privacy afforded by a trust can be invaluable, shielding sensitive financial matters from public scrutiny.

There are several types of trusts tailored to the needs of minor children. One common option is a simple trust, which distributes assets to the beneficiary at a predetermined age. This can be particularly helpful for larger inheritances, allowing for gradual distribution as the child matures and gains financial literacy. You designate a trustee, a trusted individual or institution, to manage the trust assets responsibly until the child reaches the specified age. This trustee acts as a fiduciary, legally obligated to act in the child's best interest, providing a critical layer of protection and guidance.

Another option is a Crummey trust, named after the landmark tax case that established its validity. This type of trust allows you to make annual gifts to the trust while still qualifying for the annual gift tax exclusion. Each year, the beneficiary has a limited window, typically 30 days, to withdraw the gifted amount. Although the beneficiary rarely exercises this right, the legal option to withdraw preserves the gift's tax benefits for the donor. This strategy can be particularly effective for larger estates, allowing you to reduce your taxable estate over time while ensuring the assets ultimately benefit your intended beneficiaries.

Consider, too, the benefits of a Section 2503(c) trust. This type of trust, specifically designed for minors, allows income generated within the trust to be used for the child's benefit without being taxed to the child. The trustee, again acting as a fiduciary, has the discretion to distribute funds for the child's health, education, maintenance, and support. This structure offers a valuable tax advantage while providing flexibility to address the child's evolving needs throughout their upbringing. It's a way to ensure that the inheritance is actively working for the child's well-being, not just sitting idle until they reach adulthood.

Within the context of blended families, these trust options offer even more nuanced advantages. They can help mitigate potential conflicts between step-parents and biological parents regarding inheritance. By clearly defining how assets will be distributed and managed, trusts can minimize misunderstandings and foster a smoother transition of wealth across generations. Furthermore, they can address specific family circumstances, such as providing for children from a previous marriage while ensuring the current spouse's financial security. This delicate balancing act requires careful planning, but the flexibility of trusts can provide solutions tailored to your family's unique needs.

Furthermore, trusts for minor children offer substantial protection from creditors and predators. Assets held within a trust are generally not considered part of the child's personal estate, shielding them from potential creditors or legal judgments. This protection extends even into adulthood, providing a level of financial security that can be invaluable. It's a way to safeguard the inheritance, ensuring it's used for its intended purpose, not lost to unforeseen circumstances or unscrupulous individuals.

Finally, when considering a trust for minor children, meticulous planning is paramount. Work closely with an experienced estate planning attorney. They can help you navigate the complexities of trust law, ensuring the trust document accurately reflects your wishes and complies with all applicable regulations. Selecting the right trustee is equally important. Choose someone you trust implicitly, someone with the financial acumen and integrity to manage the assets responsibly. This individual will play a pivotal role in your child's financial future, so careful consideration is essential. Building a secure financial future for your children, especially in the unique landscape of a blended family, requires proactive steps and thoughtful decision-making. Trusts for minor children offer a powerful tool to achieve that goal, providing protection, flexibility, and peace of mind for both you and your beneficiaries.

6.4 Education Planning

A comprehensive education plan is crucial in blended families, not just for the obvious benefit of securing a child's future, but also for navigating the often complex financial landscape these families present. This involves more than simply saving for college; it requires a strategic approach that considers the varying ages of children, differing educational goals, potential step-parent obligations, and the overall estate plan. Planning for education within a blended family requires careful consideration of all available resources and how they can be best utilized to meet the needs of each child while maintaining fairness and minimizing potential conflict.

One key starting point is a thorough assessment of each child's educational aspirations. This involves open conversations with the child, their biological parents, and step-parents about their interests, academic strengths, and potential career paths. Understanding these aspirations helps determine the type of education they'll likely pursue, whether it's a four-year university, vocational training, or a specialized program. This, in turn, allows for a more accurate projection of future education costs, which is fundamental to developing a sound savings plan. Furthermore, factoring in the potential impact of inflation on these costs is essential for ensuring that the funds will be sufficient when the time comes.

With a clearer picture of anticipated expenses, the next step is exploring various savings vehicles. 529 plans, for instance, offer tax-advantaged savings specifically designed for education expenses. These plans come in various forms and can be tailored to individual circumstances. Understanding the differences between prepaid tuition plans and education savings plans is vital. Prepaid tuition plans allow for the purchase of future tuition at current rates, offering a hedge against rising tuition costs, while education savings plans function more like investment accounts, growing tax-deferred and offering greater flexibility in how the funds are used. It's important to research and select the plan that best aligns with the family's risk tolerance and financial goals.

Custodial accounts, such as Uniform Transfers to Minors (UTMA) or Uniform Gifts to Minors (UGMA) accounts, present another avenue for saving. These accounts offer a simplified way to transfer assets to a minor, but it's crucial to understand their limitations. Once the child reaches the age of majority, they gain full control over the funds, regardless of their educational plans. This lack of control can be a concern in blended families where relationships may be more intricate. It's crucial to weigh the benefits and drawbacks of custodial accounts carefully within the context of the blended family dynamic.

Beyond traditional savings methods, incorporating education funding into the overall estate plan is essential. This might involve designating specific assets, such as life insurance policies or trust funds, for education purposes. Life insurance, for example, can provide a significant sum of money specifically earmarked for a child's education in the event of a parent's untimely death. Trusts offer even greater flexibility, allowing for control over how the funds are disbursed and ensuring that they're used solely for educational expenses, even after the child reaches adulthood. Within a trust, specific instructions can be laid out regarding permissible educational expenses, providing a further layer of security and control.

In blended families, where multiple children from different marriages may have varying financial needs and resources, trusts can be particularly valuable. They allow for equitable distribution of funds based on each child's specific circumstances, rather than a strict, equal division that might not address individual needs. For example, one child may be pursuing a costly medical degree, while another may choose a less expensive trade school. A trust can be structured to allocate funds accordingly, ensuring that each child has the resources they need to pursue their chosen path.

Furthermore, addressing potential step-parent obligations is a delicate but critical aspect of education planning in blended families. Open and honest discussions about financial responsibilities are crucial. While step-parents may have a strong desire to contribute to their stepchildren's education, it's essential to clarify expectations and create a plan that aligns with everyone's financial capabilities and legal obligations. These conversations should ideally occur early in the planning process, involving all relevant parties to ensure transparency and avoid future misunderstandings.

Lastly, reviewing and updating the education plan regularly is paramount.

As children grow, their interests and goals may evolve, and financial circumstances can change. Annual reviews are a good practice, providing an opportunity to adjust savings strategies, reallocate funds, and ensure the plan remains aligned with the evolving needs of the family. This ongoing review process helps maintain a dynamic and effective education plan, maximizing the benefits for all children within the blended family structure. Consistent communication, flexibility, and a proactive approach are key to navigating the intricacies of education planning in blended families and ensuring that every child has the opportunity to achieve their full potential.

6.5 Protecting Inheritance from Creditors

Safeguarding inheritances for children in blended families requires careful planning, especially when considering the potential impact of creditors. Several legal tools can be employed to create a protective barrier around these assets, ensuring they are used for the child's benefit and not subject to claims from outside parties. One primary method is establishing a trust specifically designed for the child's inheritance.

Trusts offer significant advantages in creditor protection. By placing assets within a trust, legal ownership is transferred to the trustee, who manages the funds according to the terms outlined in the trust document. This separation of ownership shields the assets from the beneficiary's creditors, as the beneficiary doesn't technically own the assets outright. Different types of trusts can be utilized, each with its own set of benefits and limitations. For example, a discretionary trust grants the trustee significant flexibility in distributing funds, allowing them to withhold distributions if the beneficiary is facing creditor issues.

Spendthrift trusts are specifically designed to protect beneficiaries from their own poor financial decisions and creditors. These trusts restrict the beneficiary's access to the principal and often limit distributions to specific purposes, like education, healthcare, or basic living expenses. The trustee's control over distributions ensures that the funds are used responsibly and aren't vulnerable to creditor claims. Another option is to establish an irrevocable trust, which offers even greater protection. Once established, the terms of an irrevocable trust cannot be easily changed, further solidifying the protection from creditors.

Beyond trusts, other legal mechanisms can provide additional layers of protection. Life insurance policies, for example, can be structured to pay out directly to a trust for the child's benefit, bypassing probate and potentially shielding the proceeds from creditors. Similarly, retirement accounts like IRAs and 401(k)s can often designate a trust as the beneficiary, ensuring the inherited funds remain protected. These designations are crucial, especially in cases where the child might be facing significant debt or legal challenges.

Prenuptial agreements also play a critical role in protecting inheritances in blended families. A well-drafted prenuptial agreement can clearly define separate property, including inheritances, and ensure it remains separate throughout the marriage and in the event of divorce. This prevents commingling of assets, which can blur the lines of ownership and make inheritances vulnerable to claims by the spouse's creditors. It's important to consult with experienced legal counsel to ensure these agreements are properly executed and legally sound.

Protecting inheritances requires not only establishing the right legal structures but also educating the beneficiaries about responsible financial management. Teaching children about budgeting, saving, and responsible debt management empowers them to make sound financial decisions and reduces the likelihood they'll face significant creditor problems in the future. Open communication about the purpose and limitations of trusts can help them understand the importance of these protective measures and foster a sense of responsibility toward their inheritance.

Beyond trusts and prenuptial agreements, asset protection planning can involve other strategies like limited liability companies (LLCs). LLCs can be used to hold assets, providing an additional layer of separation between the beneficiary and their creditors. However, it's essential to ensure the

LLC is established and operated legitimately and not used for fraudulent purposes, as this can negate the intended protections. Furthermore, certain states offer domestic asset protection trusts (DAPTs), which provide even stronger protection against creditors than traditional trusts. These trusts allow the grantor to retain some control over the assets while still shielding them from creditors. However, DAPTs are not recognized in all states, and their validity can be challenged in certain circumstances.

Properly documenting and titling assets is another key component of effective creditor protection. Ensuring that assets intended for the child's inheritance are clearly titled and designated within the trust or other protective structure is crucial. Any ambiguity in ownership can create vulnerabilities and expose the assets to potential creditor claims. Regularly reviewing and updating estate planning documents is also essential, particularly after significant life events like marriage, divorce, or the birth of a child.

Finally, seeking professional guidance from an experienced estate planning attorney is paramount. An attorney specializing in blended families and asset protection can help navigate the complexities of these situations and tailor a plan that meets the specific needs of the family. They can advise on the most appropriate legal structures, ensure proper documentation, and provide ongoing support to address any changes in circumstances or legal developments. This proactive approach safeguards the children's inheritance and provides peace of mind for the parents.

7 Navigating Family Dynamics

Open communication is the cornerstone of successful estate planning in blended families. Transparency about financial matters, estate planning decisions, and individual expectations can significantly reduce misunderstandings and potential conflicts down the line. It's crucial to foster a safe and supportive environment where all parties, including spouses, children, and stepchildren, feel comfortable expressing their concerns and asking questions. This proactive approach helps build trust and mutual understanding, essential ingredients for a harmonious family dynamic, especially when navigating sensitive financial and legacy matters. Think of these conversations not as one-time events, but as an ongoing process. Regular check-ins can help ensure everyone stays informed and aligned as circumstances evolve.

Begin by clearly articulating your own goals and intentions for your estate. What are your priorities? What kind of legacy do you envision? Sharing this information openly allows others to understand your perspective and helps frame subsequent discussions. Next, actively listen to the concerns and desires of other family members. Be empathetic and acknowledge their feelings, even if you don't agree with their viewpoints. This validation can go a long way in diffusing potential tension and fostering a sense of collaboration. Remember, the goal isn't necessarily to achieve complete consensus, but to create a shared understanding and find solutions that address everyone's core needs to the extent possible.

Consider holding family meetings dedicated specifically to estate planning matters. These structured discussions can provide a forum for open dialogue, ensuring everyone has an opportunity to be heard and contribute. Prepare an agenda beforehand to guide the conversation and stay focused on key topics. Start with less contentious issues to build momentum and create a sense of shared accomplishment. As you progress to more sensitive matters, reiterate the importance of respectful communication and active listening. Documenting key decisions and agreements reached during these meetings can be invaluable for future reference and prevent misunderstandings.

However, even with the best intentions, disagreements can arise. When communication reaches an impasse or conflicts escalate, seeking professional mediation can be a valuable resource. A skilled mediator can provide a neutral third-party perspective, facilitate constructive dialogue, and help families find mutually acceptable solutions. They can reframe issues, identify underlying interests, and guide the conversation towards compromise. Mediation can be particularly helpful in situations involving complex family dynamics, high emotional tension, or significant disagreements about asset distribution. The mediator's role is not to impose a solution, but to empower families to reach their own agreements. This collaborative approach preserves relationships and fosters a sense of ownership over the outcome.

Sometimes, disagreements may require more structured intervention. Conflict resolution strategies, often facilitated by trained professionals, can provide a framework for addressing complex family disputes. These strategies may involve a combination of negotiation, mediation, and, in some cases, arbitration. The specific approach will depend on the nature of the conflict and the willingness of the parties to engage in a collaborative process. Conflict resolution goes beyond simply resolving immediate disagreements. It aims to equip families with the skills and tools to manage future conflicts constructively.

Remember, effective communication isn't just about talking; it's about listening, empathizing, and building trust. It's about creating a space where all family members feel valued and heard. By prioritizing open communication and utilizing mediation and conflict resolution strategies when necessary, blended families can navigate the complexities of estate planning while preserving family harmony and securing their legacies for generations to come. The emotional well-being of the family is as important as the legal and financial aspects of the plan. While achieving complete agreement on every detail may be unrealistic, striving for open communication and respectful dialogue can make the process smoother and the outcome more satisfactory for everyone involved. It's an investment in both the financial future and the emotional health of the family.

7.1 Communication & Transparency

Open communication is the bedrock of successful estate planning, especially within the complex dynamics of a blended family. Transparency about financial matters, estate planning decisions, and individual expectations can significantly reduce misunderstandings and potential conflict down the line. It's not just about disclosing the existence of a will or trust, but also about explaining the reasoning behind specific provisions. Why was a certain asset allocated to a particular child? What are the long-term goals for the family's financial well-being? Answering these questions openly and honestly can foster trust and understanding among family members. Consider holding a family meeting dedicated solely to estate planning matters. This provides a structured environment for sharing information, addressing concerns, and ensuring everyone is on the same page.

Talking about money and death can be uncomfortable. However, avoiding these conversations can lead to far greater discomfort and conflict after a loved one is gone. Be prepared for a range of emotional responses. Some family members might feel apprehensive about discussing their own mortality, while others might be concerned about perceived favoritism or inequitable distribution of assets. Patience and empathy are crucial. Acknowledge these feelings and create a safe space for open dialogue where everyone feels comfortable expressing their thoughts and concerns. Remember, the goal is not necessarily to achieve complete agreement, but rather to foster mutual understanding and respect.

Transparency extends beyond simply sharing information; it also involves actively listening and responding to concerns. If a stepchild feels excluded from the estate plan, or a biological child questions the provisions made for their step-siblings, address those concerns directly and honestly. Explain the rationale behind the decisions, emphasizing the overall goals for the family's financial security. Perhaps a specific provision was designed to protect a child with special needs, or to ensure the continuity of a family business. Sharing this context can help alleviate anxieties and foster a sense of fairness. Remember, even if complete agreement isn't possible, clear and respectful communication can significantly reduce the potential for future disputes.

One particularly sensitive area within blended families is the distribution of personal belongings with sentimental value. These items often carry significant emotional weight, and their allocation can be a source of contention. Openly discussing the distribution of these items before they become points of conflict can prevent misunderstandings and hurt feelings. Consider creating a separate list or addendum to the will or trust specifically addressing the distribution of sentimental items. This allows for greater clarity and reduces the likelihood of disputes arising from assumptions or differing interpretations. Family members might even consider participating in the process of assigning sentimental value and preferred recipients, fostering a sense of shared responsibility and understanding.

Consider engaging a neutral third party, such as an estate planning attorney or a family therapist specializing in financial matters, to facilitate these conversations. A skilled professional can provide guidance, mediate disagreements, and ensure that all perspectives are heard and respected. They can also offer objective insights and suggest strategies for addressing complex family dynamics. This can be especially helpful if pre-existing tensions or communication challenges exist within the family. The neutral party can create a structured environment where everyone feels safe to express their thoughts and concerns, fostering a more productive and less emotionally charged discussion.

Estate planning is not a one-time event but rather an ongoing process that requires regular review and updates. As family circumstances change – marriages, births, divorces, deaths – the estate plan should be revisited and adjusted accordingly. These changes can significantly impact the distribution of assets and the overall effectiveness of the estate plan. Open communication should continue throughout this process, ensuring that all family members are aware of any updates and understand the rationale behind them. Regular communication also helps maintain transparency and minimizes the potential for surprises or disputes in the future.

Building a strong foundation of communication and transparency is a crucial investment in the long-term well-being of a blended family. It fosters trust, reduces conflict, and ensures that the estate plan effectively reflects the family's values and goals. While navigating these sensitive conversations can be challenging, the rewards – in terms of family harmony and financial security – are immeasurable. By prioritizing open dialogue, active listening, and mutual respect, blended families can create a more secure and harmonious future for all members. This proactive approach to communication can transform estate planning from a potential source of conflict into an opportunity for strengthening family bonds and ensuring everyone's needs are met.

7.2 Mediation & Conflict Resolution

Blended families, by their very nature, often involve complex emotional ties and pre-existing financial structures. These complexities can easily escalate into conflict, especially when addressing sensitive topics like inheritance and estate planning. Understanding how to navigate these potential conflicts through mediation and other conflict resolution techniques is crucial for preserving family harmony and ensuring a smooth estate administration process. Successfully navigating these challenging conversations requires careful planning, empathy, and a willingness to compromise.

Open communication forms the cornerstone of effective conflict resolution. Families should strive to create a safe and respectful environment where each member feels comfortable expressing their concerns and desires. This often involves scheduling dedicated family meetings, perhaps with a neutral facilitator, to discuss estate planning goals and address any potential points of contention. Transparency about assets, liabilities, and estate planning decisions is essential to building trust and minimizing misunderstandings. Remember, effective communication isn't just about talking; it's also about actively listening and acknowledging the perspectives of others, even if you don't agree with them.

Mediation can be an invaluable tool when family discussions reach an impasse. A skilled mediator, often an attorney or therapist specializing in family matters, can provide a neutral third-party perspective and facilitate constructive dialogue. The mediator's role isn't to impose a solution but rather to guide the family toward a mutually agreeable resolution. They help identify the underlying interests and needs of each party, fostering a collaborative problem-solving approach. Mediation offers a structured environment for addressing complex emotional dynamics and can significantly reduce the likelihood of escalating disputes.

Beyond formal mediation, families can employ various conflict resolution strategies in their everyday interactions. Active listening, where individuals demonstrate genuine interest in understanding each other's viewpoints, is a powerful technique for de-escalating tension. Empathy, the ability to understand and share the feelings of others, plays a vital role in fostering compassion and finding common ground. Learning to reframe issues in a less confrontational manner can also contribute to a more productive dialogue. For example, instead of focusing on individual positions, try to identify shared goals and values. This shift in perspective can help bridge divides and facilitate compromise.

Conflict can sometimes arise from differing interpretations of legal or financial matters. In such cases, seeking professional advice from estate planning attorneys, tax advisors, or financial planners can be beneficial. These professionals can provide objective information and clarify complex legal and financial concepts, helping families make informed decisions and avoid misunderstandings. Having a clear understanding of the legal and tax implications of various estate planning options can empower families to make choices that align with their collective goals.

Documentation is a critical component of successful conflict resolution. Once agreements are reached, it's essential to document them clearly and concisely. This might involve revising estate planning documents, creating memorandums of understanding, or simply keeping detailed records of family meetings. Clear documentation helps prevent future disputes by providing a tangible record of the agreed-upon terms. This clarity minimizes ambiguity and ensures that everyone is on the same page regarding the estate plan's implementation.

While focusing on resolution is paramount, it's equally important to acknowledge that not all family conflicts can be entirely resolved. Sometimes, despite best efforts, irreconcilable differences may persist. In such situations, families may need to explore alternative strategies, such as establishing clear boundaries to minimize interaction or seeking legal counsel to protect individual rights and interests. While these outcomes may not be ideal, they can provide a necessary framework for managing ongoing disagreements and preserving some level of family cohesion.

Building strong family relationships requires ongoing effort and a commitment to open communication, empathy, and compromise. By proactively addressing potential conflicts through mediation and other resolution techniques, blended families can navigate the complexities of estate planning while preserving family harmony and ensuring a smooth transition of wealth across generations. This proactive approach not only minimizes the potential for legal disputes but also strengthens family bonds by fostering trust and mutual respect. Ultimately, a well-crafted estate plan, combined with effective conflict resolution strategies, can provide peace of mind and a lasting legacy for blended families. Remember that seeking professional guidance from experienced estate planning attorneys and mediators is essential for navigating these complexities and achieving positive outcomes for all involved.

www.ingramcontent.com/pod-product-compliance
Lightning Source LLC
LaVergne TN
LVHW022022200926
848481LV00007B/2490